BY THE AUTHOR


*Poetry*
The Plain People
Between Root and Sky
The Maidenhair Tree
Ships in Bottles
Walking to Santiago
The Road to the Gunpowder House
Other Rooms (Selected Poems)
Some Letters Never Sent
On Keeping Company With Mrs Woolf


*Translations*
Euripides, The Bacchae
Euripides, The Trojan Women
Euripides, The Helen
Homer, The Bending of the Bow
Jules Supervielle, The Fable of the World
The Dream of the Rood


*Criticism*
Norman Nicholson
Christopher Smart
George Herbert (co-written with Natasha Curry)
Alexander Pope
Six Eighteenth-century Poets
William Cowper: a Revaluation


*Topography*
The Cumberland Coast

# WILLIAM SHENSTONE

# WILLIAM SHENSTONE

landscape gardener and poet

## NEIL CURRY

GE

Greenwich Exchange
London

Greenwich Exchange, London

First published in Great Britain in 2020
All rights reserved

William Shenstone: Landscape Gardener and Poet
© Neil Curry, 2020

Printed and bound by imprintdigital.com
Cover design by December Publications
Tel: 07951511275

Greenwich Exchange Website: www.greenex.co.uk

Cover: Portrait of William Shenstone by Edward Alcock
(Photo by Birmingham Museums Trust, licensed under CC0)

Cataloguing in Publication Data is available
from the British Library

ISBN: 978-1-910996-34-8

# CONTENTS

1 *L'Allegro* 11

2 The Warwickshire Coterie *23*

3 The Poet *44*

4 The Essayist *75*

5 The Editor *89*

6 The Letter-Writer *111*

7 The Landscape Gardener *132*

8 *Il Penseroso? 156*

Bibliography

Index

# 1

# L'ALLEGRO

THE POEM WITH WHICH ROGER LONSDALE chose to open his acclaimed anthology, *The New Oxford Book of Eighteenth Century Verse*, was *The Choice* by John Pomfret. 'Of Mr John Pomfret nothing is known...' is how Johnson began his brief life of him and yet, paradoxically, he then went on to say that, 'Perhaps no composition in our language has been oftener perused than Pomfret's *Choice*'[1] and even in 1807 we find a bewildered Robert Southey asking, 'Why is Pomfret the most popular of the English poets?' Today both the man and his poem are largely forgotten, but when it first appeared in 1700 *The Choice* struck a chord which resonated with all its readers and long continued to do so. The tranquil life it celebrated was exactly what people felt they wanted after the excesses of the previous century, with its religious strife, the bloodshed of civil war, the execution of one king and the rejection of another, added to which was all the brouhaha which had come in with the restoration of Charles II. Small wonder then

---

[1]Samuel Johnson, *Lives of the English Poets*, ed G.B. Hill (London, 1905) Vol III, p302

that so many thought how fine it would be to opt out, to leave the court and the city and enjoy a more peaceful existence in the country. But for most people, with a living to earn, or an ambition to follow, this was little more than a dream. It was in fact a dream for Pomfret too, as we can see from the opening word of his poem: 'If … '

The idealisation of rural life was nothing new; it had the whole of the Virgilian pastoral tradition behind it, plus, of course, and famously, Horace's second epode in which Alfius the money-lender, albeit satirically, is made to assert that:

> Beatus ille, qui procul negotiis
> > ut prisca gens mortalium,
> paterna rura bubus exercet suis
> > solutus omni faenore;

Lines which Philip Francis, just one of countless eighteenth-century translators, rendered in 1742 as:

> Like the first mortals blest is he
> > From debts, and mortgages, and business free,
> With his own team who ploughs the soil
> > Which grateful once confest his father's toil.

In addition to the numerous translations, there were imitations and echoes of these lines to be found everywhere: two outstanding instances being Ben Jonson's warm tribute to the way of life he had enjoyed at Penshurst and Andrew Marvell's enchanting lines on the 'fair quiet' and 'wond'rous life' he had experienced in his own garden.

But the exoticism of Marvell and the luxury and abundance we read of in Jonson were both rejected by Pomfret. It is eighteenth-century moderation which his neatly balanced couplets extol. The house of *his* dreams would be a modest one and certainly sport no gaudy furnishings.

Near some fair town I'd have a private seat,
Built uniform, not little, nor too great:
Better, if on a rising ground it stood,
Fields on this side, on that a neighbouring wood.
It should within no other things contain,
But what were useful, necessary, plain.                    (5-10)

It would have a little garden with a 'cool rivulet' running through it, and an avenue of lime trees

At th'end of which a silent study placed
Should be with all the noblest authors graced.             (17-18)

He had, he tells us, no wish to be rich, but would be content if:

A frugal plenty should my table spread,
With healthy, not luxurious dishes, fed.                    (44-45)

And, charitably, with enough left over so that he could 'feed the stranger and the neighbouring poor'.

He would not deny himself 'a little vault … with the best wines each vintage could afford', but assured his readers that there would be no over-indulgence in his house. The hedonism of Restoration England was something he firmly rebuffed.

Friends would be welcome, as long as they met the lengthy list of virtues he set out for them, so would a lady friend, the qualities asked of her being equally demanding. This, however, was one wish which landed him in deep trouble, for, as he did not want her living *with* him ('for I'd have no wife', he declared), he seemed to be advocating having a mistress: 'To this fair creature I'd sometimes retire/Her conversation would new joys inspire.' The Bishop of London, who knew that Pomfret was married, nevertheless decided to interpret it in such a way and, to be fair to him, 'conversation' was a word which did have sexual overtones at that time. As a result, any hope of preferment the Reverend Mr Pomfret might have had in the church was at an end, and as he died in 1702, he did not live to see his *Poems* go through edition after edition.

Pomfret's classically educated readers would have recognised the Horatian ideal which lay behind the day dreams in the first half of the poem. In fact its opening lines are very close to those of *Satire* II.6, as can be seen from the translation by Christopher Smart:

> This was the summit of my views,
> A little piece of land to use,
> Where was a garden and a well,
> Near to the house in which I dwell,
> And something of a wood above.

However, the eighteenth-century notion of the Horatian ideal is perhaps most clearly presented to us in Alexander Pope's 'Ode on Solitude'.

> Happy the man, whose wish and care
> A few paternal acres bound,
> Content to breathe his native air,
>         In his own ground.
>
> Whose herds with milk, whose fields with bread,
> Whose flocks supply him with attire,
> Whose trees in summer yield him shade,
>         In winter fire.
>
> Blest! who can unconcern'dly find
> Hours, days, and years slide soft away,
> In health of body, peace of mind,
>         Quiet by day.
>
> Sound sleep by night; study and ease
> Together mix'd; sweet recreation,
> And innocence, which most does please,
>         With Meditation.

Thus let me live, unseen, unknown;
Thus unlamented let me dye;
Steal from the world, and not a stone
        Tell where I lye.

Pope's youthful literary antennae had detected the groundswell of a new movement, one to which Addison had put his powerful stamp of approval in *The Spectator*.

True Happiness is of a retired Nature and an Enemy to Pomp and Noise; it arises in the first place, from the Enjoyment of ones self; and, in the next, from the Friendship and Conversation of a few select Companions. It loves Shade and Solitude, and naturally haunts Groves and Fountains, Fields and Meadows. In short, it feels everything it wants within itself, and receives no Addition from Multitudes of Witnesses and Spectators. (Number 15, March 1711)

This was then endorsed by James Thomson throughout his poem 'The Seasons':

An elegant sufficiency, content,
Retirement, rural quiet, friendship, books,
Ease and alternate labour, useful life,
Progressive virtue, and approving Heaven!
These are the matchless joys
(*Spring* 1159-1163)

Before long the theme is everywhere you look and the popular journals of the day are filled with such *wishful-thinking* poetry. And it was not a theme only for poetry. It is to be found in the novels too. In *Joseph Andrews* Fielding records for us the rural contentment enjoyed by Mr Wilson, and that of Squire Allworthy in *Tom Jones*. Added to which is the life lived by that most sweet-natured of clerics, Dr Primrose, the Vicar of Wakefield, and Goldsmith's description of his little estate is as close as can be to Horace's *Satire* and the opening lines of *The Choice*,

> Our little habitation was situated at the foot of a sloping hill, sheltered
> with a beautiful underwood behind and a prattling river before; on
> one side a meadow, on the other a green.
>
> (Ch. 4)

There are many possible reasons for this flowering of interest in
the Horatian dream. The towns and cities were growing at an
unprecedented rate and the pollution becoming such that those
members of the rising merchant class who could afford to move
out did so, but mostly they moved into the type of villa which
William Cowper was to describe rather contemptuously in his poem
*Retirement*:

> Suburban villas, highway-side retreats
> That dread th'encroachment of our growing streets,
> Tight boxes, neatly sash'd, and in a blaze
> With all a July sun's collected rays
> Delight the citizen, who gasping there
> Breathes clouds of dust and calls it country air.    (481-486)

It was also the time when great country estates were being
designed, at Castle Howard and Blenheim, at Stourhead and Stowe.
But their vast parks were no more Horatian than were the suburban
villas, and Pope, we can be sure, had no more wish to live 'unknown'
and in solitude than Thomson wished for retirement and rural
quiet. It was all a pleasing fantasy, a classically-inspired literary
genre. And yet, there was one man who did deliberately and
consciously lead such a life. He was William Shenstone.

\* \* \* \*

Before looking closely into Shenstone's many interests and
achievements, a brief outline of his life may, as Robert Dodsley, his
first editor, put it, 'not only be agreeable, but absolutely necessary

to the reader'. He was born on 18 November 1714, 'the eldest son,' as Dodsley goes on to tell us, 'of a plain, uneducated country gentlemen, who farmed his own estate.' That estate was The Leasowes, near Halesowen, which in the early years of the eighteenth century was not yet a suburb of Birmingham, but a small market town. The country gentleman was Thomas Shenstone who had married well, his wife being Ann Penn, one of the Penns of nearby Harborough Hall, and so a family entitled to regard themselves as gentry.

Thomas Shenstone may himself have been 'uneducated' (a term which probably meant only that he had not been to university) but he took care to educate his two sons. The fact that William's first school was a Dame School would be unremarkable were it not that he wrote so movingly of it and of Sarah Lloyd, the Dame herself, in his most celebrated poem 'The Schoolmistress'. In it we read of her threatening her young charges with the birch and then giving them sweets if she did happen to use it.

Next came Solihull School, where he met his lifelong friend, the poet Richard Jago, and where, under the guidance of the Rev William Crumpton, he acquired a thorough grounding in the Classics, and also, which was rather unusual for the times, where he was introduced to English literature, notably Edmund Spenser. From there, in 1732, he went up to Pembroke College, Oxford, which Samuel Johnson, who had left there the year before, was later to tell Boswell was 'a nest of singing birds'.

It was expected that an Oxford degree would lead to ordination and a career in the church, but that was not to be. His father had died when William was at Solihull and his mother in the year that he went up to Oxford. Then the death of his maternal uncle and guardian, Thomas Dolman, in the year that he reached his majority meant that he inherited The Leasowes and an income of £300 a year from his share in the Harborough property. A brief visit to his new estate was enough to convince him that life there would be far better than having to work at Oxford and though he did keep his name on the college books for some years he never resumed his studies. Gainful employment does not seem to have crossed his mind as an option either, as his friend, Richard Graves, who knew him well, explained, 'Indolence persuades him … that it was better to enjoy ease and independence with a competent fortune, than to toil, and be subject to the caprice of others, to augment it.'[2] Three hundred pounds e a year was not a fortune, but as it was about twice the sum on which many a clergyman was then supporting a family. Life at The Leasowes, while never luxurious, would know few hardships.

He did go back briefly to Oxford in 1737, but only to organise the printing of his first collection, *Poems On Various Occasions*. It was subtitled 'Written for the Entertainment of the Author and printed for the Amusement of a few Friends Prejudic'd in his Favour'. It is noteworthy for the inclusion of an early version of 'The Schoolmistress', but Shenstone ceased to be entertained by it and went to great lengths to collect and destroy copies whenever he could lay hands on them. As a result, it is now a very rare book indeed.

As The Leasowes had been let to another branch of the Shenstone family at that time, he had gone to live at nearby Harborough Hall, where he was joined by Richard Graves, who described the month they spent together there as a time passed 'in a very agreeable loiter'.[3] They wandered about the grounds, and sat in the summer-house reading Boileau 'and other French critics or entertaining authors; and Mr Shenstone wrote several little pieces of poetry'. It was the type of life which he was to grow used to.

---

[2] Richard Graves, *Recollections of some Particulars in the Life of the late William Shenstone, Esq* (London, 1788), p35
[3] ibid, p36

In 1788, a quarter of a century after Shenstone's death, Graves
had begun his *Recollections of some Particulars in the Life of the
late William Shenstone, Esq* by stating that he had lived 'a life of
such absolute sequestration from the busy world'.[4] But this is
certainly not true of his early twenties. On a return visit to Graves's
house in the village of Mickleton in Gloucestershire, he is said to
have fallen in love with Richard's sister, Mary. Sadly, his love was
not returned. Nevertheless her brother declared, perhaps rather
teasingly, that it was a passion 'at least on the sensibility of Mr
Shenstone, which, I believe, took entire possession of his heart for
some years'.[5] This is open to question though as we are told that he
was also attracted to a Miss Carter while staying in Cheltenham.
Added to this we know that he and Graves both fell in love with
Utrecia Smith, the daughter of a local curate and a young woman,
according to Graves, of outstanding 'learning and ingenuity'.

Shenstone's feet were as unsettled as his heart at this time, it
would seem, as we hear of him attending concerts in Birmingham
and at Worcester, where he was delighted by a performance of
Handel's *Messiah.* Then there were the extended visits he made to
London, which he clearly enjoyed. In November 1741 he is urging
Richard Jago to join him: 'Let me have the pleasure of seeing you
in the pit, in a laughter as cordial and singular as your friendship.
Come – let us go forth into the opera-house; let us hear how the
eunuch-folk sing. Turn your eye upon the lilies and roses, diamonds
and rubies; the Belindas and the Sylvias of gay life!' He was not
unaware of the darker side of the capital though, and in February
1743, he is admitting, again to Jago, that 'London is really dangerous
… the pickpockets formerly content with mere filching, make no

[4]ibid, p3
[5]ibid, p47

scruple to knock people down with bludgeons in Fleet Street and the Strand, and that at no later hour than 8 o'clock.'[6]

But London was where any aspiring writer needed to be in the middle years of the eighteenth century and Shenstone had managed to make his mark there. In April 1741 his long poem 'The Judgement of Hercules' was published by Robert Dodsley, who also published a separate edition of 'The Schoolmistress' in the following year. By the time he visited Cheltenham in 1743 he was recognised as Shenstone the poet, and it was there that he began work on his 'Pastoral Ballad'.

Shenstone's life then underwent a change which was to establish his reputation in an altogether different direction. In March 1743 he wrote to Richard Jago, 'I am taking part of my farm upon my hands, to see if I can succeed as a farmer.'[7] He never did succeed as a farmer; instead he became one of the most respected and influential landscape-gardeners in the country, and, according to the OED, the first person ever to use the term 'landscape-gardening'. In all his gardening schemes he was aided and encouraged by Lady Henrietta Luxborough, a vivacious and highly intelligent woman with something of a chequered past and who, although some fifteen years his senior, became one of his closest friends and a tireless correspondent.

Samuel Johnson, a metropolitan through and through, doubted whether landscape-gardening was an occupation which 'demands any great powers of mind', nevertheless he conceded that Shenstone had 'judgement and such fancy as made his little domain the envy of the great and the admiration of the skilful: a place to be visited by travellers, and copied by designers.'[8] By 1759, such was the fame

---

[6]Marjorie Williams, ed, *The Letters of William Shenstone* (Oxford, 1939)
[7]ibid, p85
[8]Johnson, Vol III, p359

of The Leasowes that Shenstone began one of his letters to Jago, 'It is now Sunday evening, and I have been exhibiting myself in my walks to no less than a hundred and fifty people, and that with no less state and vanity than a Turk in his seraglio.'[9]

And it was not only in landscape-gardening that Shenstone was regarded as an arbiter of taste and judgement. He had, after some early disagreements, become a close friend of his publisher Robert Dodsley, and when Dodsley was at work on his *Collection of Poems by Several Hands,* which was to become the definitive anthology of the century, it was to Shenstone that he turned when he felt the need for assistance and advice. Hence several of Shenstone's close friends – Jago, Graves, Somerville and Whistler – are included. The six volumes were eventually to feature all the most famous poets of the age: Pope, Gray, Thomson, Collins and Johnson, and such was Dodsley's estimation of his friend's work that the first 60 pages of Volume IV are devoted entirely to Shenstone.

This was not the only publication Shenstone was involved with. When Dodsley was staying with him at The Leasowes in 1757 they were visited by a young man who had brought with him a folio of old ballads which he had found. Macpherson's 'Ossian' had recently caused a publicity stir and Dodsley and Shenstone were not slow to see the opportunity that this new discovery presented. The young man was Thomas Percy and over the next few years Shenstone helped him to search out and edit what we now know as *Percy's Reliques of Ancient English Poetry,* a book which was to have a powerful influence on Wordsworth and Coleridge in their younger and formative years, leading them towards their own *Lyrical Ballads* and the rise of Romanticism.

Sadly, while Percy acknowledged Shenstone's assistance in his

---

[9]Williams *Letters,* p204

Preface, he also had to record that 'The plan of the work was settled in concert with the late elegant Mr Shenstone, who was to have borne a joint share in it had not death unhappily prevented him.'

In the *Arts Gazette* it was recorded that, 'On Friday 11th February 1763, after a short but violent fever which he bore with philosophic fortitude and a Christian resignation, dy'd aged 48, William Shenstone Esq. of The Leasowes: the pride of his country, the favourite of the muses, and what still redounds to his praise, the enemy of vice and the friend of virtue.'

To his great credit, Robert Dodsley – who himself was not in the best of health – spent the last years of his life putting together and publishing Shenstone's Collected Works. They are elegant volumes. The first contains all his poetry. In the second we find a collection of his essays, many of which will bear comparison with any of the best essay-writers of the time. Added to these is a collection of witty and perceptive aphorisms and his letters make up the third volume.

Having achieved more than most people ever do, and in so many different fields – gardener-designer, poet, essayist and letter-writer – Shenstone deserves to be remembered. And in addition he is also credited by the OED with the first usage of what was claimed to be the longest word in the language: floccinaucinihilipilification – no mean achievement in itself.

# 2

# THE WARWICKSHIRE COTERIE

*FLOCCI-NAUCI-NIHILI-PILI-FICATION* WAS used by Shenstone as a term of approval in a letter he wrote in July 1742 to tell Richard Jago of the death of their friend, the poet William Somervile. It means regarding something as of little value or importance. Shenstone had written, 'I loved him for nothing so much as his flocci-nauci-nihili-pili-fication of money.'[1] This is recorded as the first *use* of the word, but as in the *Eton Latin Grammar*, the list of verbs which govern the genitive begins: *flocci, nauci, nihili, pili*. It may well have had previous history as a joke among classically-educated schoolboys.

The Somerviles of Edstone Hall, situated a few miles north of Stratford, were a very well-respected Warwickshire family who could trace their lineage back to an ancestor who had fought with William the Conqueror. William Somervile, the poet, had been educated at Winchester and elected Fellow of New College Oxford, but as Johnson laconically records, 'It does not appear that in the

---

[1] Marjorie Williams, ed, *The Letters of William Shenstone* (Oxford, 1939), p56

places of his education he exhibited any uncommon proofs of genius or literature.'[2] He did, however, concede, albeit rather laconically, that 'It may commonly be said that he *writes very well for a gentleman.*'

In his early days he had composed odes to celebrity figures such as the Duke of Marlborough, Addison, Pope and Thomson, but, to quote Johnson again, 'His subjects are commonly such as require no great depth of thought, or energy of expression,' and do tend to make us see what Robert Graves meant when he dubbed those years 'The Age of Obsequiousness'.

Nevertheless, a gentleman he most certainly was, and like many another gentleman of his time his chief passion was hunting, and when he was not hunting then his next delight was playing bowls, and both were topics he wrote about at some length. His poem 'The Bowling Green' runs to 700 couplets, but has some lively moments, as well as some entertaining portraits of his fellow bowlers, especially that of the local parish priest, whom he dubs Zadoc.

> Next Zadoc 'tis thy turn, imperious priest,
> Still late at church, but early at the feast …
> He grasps the bowl in his rough brawny hand,
> Then squatting down, with his great goggle eyes
> He takes his aim, and at the mark it flies.
> Zadoc pursues and wobbles o'er the plain,
> But shakes his strutting paunch and ambles on in vain.

Having hunted, it is believed, almost every day of his life, he decided, when he was nearing 60 and finding that infirmity now confined him to his elbow-chair, that he would write 'The Chase', even if he could no longer follow it.

---

[2]Samuel Johnson, *Lives of the English Poets*, Vol II, p317

Johnson would only go so far as to grant that 'To this poem praise cannot be totally denied.'[3] But it is as vigorous a poem as Somervile himself had once been, one which quickly met with a good deal of success and which was still being printed in the early years of the following century, and understandably so, as he not only displays his passion for hunting; he also has much to tell us about it. In some respects it may be viewed as a Georgic. In Book One he tells us exactly where and how kennels should be built, and stresses the need to keep them clean.

> Soon as the growling pack with eager joy
> Have lapp'd their smoking viands, morn or eve,
> From the full cistern lead the ductile streams,
> To wash thy court well-pav'd, nor spare thy pains,
> For much to health will cleanliness avail.          (154-158)

The diction is conventional in a way which grates somewhat on us today, but convention is a coming together, a cultural conformity, and therefore a word which ought to indicate that it was what people wanted and expected. To fault it is tantamount to complaining that there are too many murders today on television.

Somervile's diction in no way disguises the violence and bloodthirstiness of the sport, an aspect which he appears to have enjoyed.

> The huntsman now, a deep incision made,
> Shakes out with hands impure, and dashes down
> Her reeking entrails, and yet quiv'ring heart.
> These claim the pack, the bloody perquisite
> For all their toils. Stretch'd on the ground she lies
> A mangled corpse.                                    (281-287)

It is surprising that Shenstone was prepared to accept this in a

---

[3]ibid, p319

friend, as in one of his *Essays on Men, Manners and Things*, he wrote, 'The world may be divided into people that read, people that write, people that think, and fox-hunters.'[4] But as one of Somervile's editors observed, 'Our author was highly regarded by all his contemporaries for his great benevolence and affability of disposition.'[5] Sadly, this affability got out of control. The ensuing debts meant that he had to borrow money from a wealthy relative, putting up his entire estate as security, but still the debts mounted, then debt led to anxiety, anxiety to drink and the drink to his death. Shenstone was greatly distressed by it all and his letter to Jago began:

> Our old friend Somervile is dead! I did not imagine I could have been so sorry as I find myself on this occasion. I can now excuse all his foibles; impute them to age, and to distress of circumstances: the last of these considerations wrings my very soul to think on. For a man of high spirit, conscious of having (at least in one production) generally pleased the world, to be plagued and threatened by wretches that are low in every sense; to be forced to drink himself into pains of the body in order to get rid of the pains of the mind, is a misery which I can well conceive.[6]

Though it took them several years to complete the scheme, his friends rallied round to provide a memorial to him. It was to be in the grounds of his neighbour, Lady Luxborough, to commemorate her 'great esteem for him who was a worthy Man and a good Poet, who honoured me with his friendship'.[7] Dozens of letters passed between her and Shenstone as they debated, over and over again, its exact size, shape and position. Eventually it was decided to erect an urn at the foot of a double oak where Shenstone and Somervile had first met. Neatly combining the great loves of his life, it was

---

[4]William Shenstone, *Works in Verse and Prose* (London, 1769) Vol II, p170
[5]William Somervile, *The Chase*, ed Edward Topham (London, 1817), p16
[6]*Letters*, p55-56
[7]ibid, p176

decorated with a hunting horn surrounded by a laurel wreath. Shenstone's own memorial to his friend is contained in his Elegy XVIII.

Near-neighbours as they were, the friendship between Somervile and Lady Luxborough went back many years. They were, it might be claimed, the founders of what was to become known as the Warwickshire Coterie, a group, centred on Lady Luxborough's house, The Barrells in Ullenhall, and which included Shenstone, Jago, Graves and Whistler. None as writers could be regarded as being of the first grade, but that is no disgrace. As Shenstone himself observed in one of his aphorisms, 'What numbers live to the age of fifty or sixty years, yet if estimated by their merit, are not worth the price of a chick the moment it is hatched.'[8] The members of the Warwickshire Coterie merited more highly than that and if we consider them carefully we find we are seeing a different and not invalid picture of their times.

Not every eighteenth-century writer was a celebrity. They did not all live in London where, as Pope put it:

> With varying Vanities, from ev'ry Part,
> They shift the moving Toyshop of their Heart;
> Where Wigs with Wigs, with Sword-knots Sword-knots strive,
> Beaus banish Beaus, and Coaches Coaches drive.
>
> (*The Rape of the Lock*, I. 99-103)

Shenstone, for one, never wore a wig and neither he nor any of his friends could be held guilty of the follies and extravagancies satirized by Pope and Swift. They were people who, dismissed as provincials by the Wits of the City, were, it could be argued, rather more in touch with the central energies and patterns of their time. They were the norm, and in the life story of Lady Luxborough we

---

[8]*Works*, II, p220

see, sadly, what was all too often looked upon as normal in the way women were treated in the middle years of the eighteenth century.

Born Henrietta St John in 1699, she had some colourful antecedents. One of her great aunts was Lady Castlemaine, mistress to Charles II. An uncle was the dissolute poet and rake Lord Rochester, who had managed to drink himself to death by the age of 32. Her own father had killed a man in a drunken tavern brawl; found guilty and sentenced to be hanged at Tyburn he had managed to escape to France, later paying Charles the hefty sum of £16,000 to be allowed to return home. Her father-in-law had been cashier to the notorious South Sea Company and had also made a rapid escape to France with a good deal of other people's money. And her eldest brother, Lord St John Bolingbroke, the close friend of Alexander Pope, was credited by Swift with 'drinking like a fish and fucking like a goat'.[9] He too had to flee to France after his involvement in the Jacobite uprising of 1715. Yet the lady herself, guilty of little more than an indiscretion, was cast aside by her husband and ostracised by 'polite society'.

There was a 21 year age-gap between Henrietta and her brother and, to his credit, he seems to have taken upon himself her education, both intellectual and social. As a young woman, she was a frequent guest at Dawley, his elegant Queen Anne mansion near Uxbridge. It was here that he played host to the likes of Alexander Pope, John Gay and the beautiful and fashionable Duchess of Queensbury. Henrietta was accustomed therefore to being surrounded by luxury, but also by ideas: discussions of poetry and politics, music and philosophy. Renowned for her wit and vitality, she could hold her own on such occasions, added to which,

---

[9]Audrey Duggan, *Chequered Changes: A Portrait of Lady Luxborough* (Brewin Books, 2008), p83

as we can see from the portrait painted of her by the Swedish artist Michael Dahl, she was very beautiful, calm, self-assured, and with a luxuriant mass of shoulder-length dark brown hair. So it is rather surprising that she did not marry until she was 28 and her choice of Robert Knight was a surprise too. He was never her intellectual equal. 'A little wizen husband,' was what the waspish Horace Walpole called him. Money – ill-gotten South Sea Bubble money – was probably an issue, but she does seem to have loved him. However, much of her married life was spent in France where her father-in-law, who had been heavily implicated in the scandal, was seeking to re-establish his reputation. It was a life of social entertaining and where, as she wrote to a friend, 'the pleasures of the mind are denied'.[10] But on her visits to England such pleasures could be found again at Marlborough Castle in the company of her friends, the Somerset poet Elizabeth Rowe, and Frances, Countess of Hertford, who was to become patron to James Thomson. All three shared an interest in poetry and also, it would seem, in Mr John Dalton, a handsome young clergyman, Oxford educated, who was employed as tutor to the Hertfords' son. He joined them on their walks, in their discussions and in their exchanges of witty rhyming letters. It was a game – a little flirtatious, perhaps – but some of his verses do make us stop and wonder.

> Give me the Friendship of my Fair;
> Give me that something still more Dear –
> In Love's light Plumes be others drest
> I ask no more – than to be blest.

But when a letter from Dalton was discovered by her husband he did more than wonder. It was probably, as she protested, only a piece of silliness, but when rumours – probably sparked by Walpole

---

[10]ibid, p28

– began to circulate, that was too much for him. Divorce was complex and difficult at that time, but the marriage was over. As Richard Graves so coyly puts it, she was no longer 'living on terms of the most perfect conjugal felicity with her Lord'. In fact he had offered her two choices. The first was that she could remain in the family home, but be locked away in the attics, denied pen, paper or books and not even allowed into the garden. It was a choice which at first she accepted, but could not sustain. Who could? A poem titled 'The Bullfinch in Town' suggests that she fully understood the effects of imprisonment.

> And while to please some courtly fair,
>     He one dull tune with labour learns,
> A well-gilt cage remote from air,
>     And faded plumes, is all he earns!
>
> Go, hapless captive! still repeat
>     The sounds which nature never taught;
> Go, listening fair! and call them sweet,
>     Because you know them dearly bought.

Indeed, she had written to a friend, 'Liberty is so sweet that it is more natural for me to choose ... a remote cottage free, than to remain at home a prisoner.'[11] That was the second choice she had been given. The Barrells, near Henley-in-Arden, was a farmhouse, not a cottage, but it was hardly habitable. Considering her upbringing, one might have thought that faced with a building so remote and without a full set of doors and windows, Henrietta might have fallen into despair. Instead, she began a new life. Granted that her husband allowed her £500 a year (£200 more than Shenstone ever had) and, even if sometimes rather grudgingly, paid

---

[11] ibid, p38

for the improvements, she transformed a hovel into a gracious home and established a garden to rival The Leasowes, complete with a summer house and an avenue of lime trees. And when her husband was raised to the peerage she ceased to be Mrs Knight and became, probably to his chagrin, Lady Luxborough.

On her first taking up residence there, the ladies of the area avoided having any contact with her. She was a fallen woman, and her reputation was to take a further blow two decades later when her daughter left her husband and eloped to France with her lover, Sir Joshua Childs. But the local clergy had made her welcome from the start – one in particular, Shenstone's old school friend, the Rev Richard Jago – and so the Warwickshire Coterie began and she soon had around her a gathering, if not quite so glamorous, at least reminiscent of those times she had spent at her brother's house all those years before.

Richard Jago was born in 1715 in Beaudesert, Henley-in-Arden, where his father was the rector. Beaudesert is only a few miles north of Edstone, the home of William Somervile who, though 40 years older than Jago, read his early poems and generously gave him some encouragement and advice, as we learn from the first book of Jago's long poem 'Edge Hill'.

> O Beaudesert! old Montfort's lofty seat
> Haunt of my youthful steps! where I was wont
> To range, chanting my rude notes to the wind,
> While Somervile disdained not to regard,
> With candid ear, and regulate the strain.

His youthful steps took him to Solihull School where he found himself in the same class as William Shenstone, who was to be his friend for life. They were taught by a Mr Crompton, who, in addition to Latin and Greek, gave them an early taste for the English classics, which was rather unusual in those days. But Mr Crompton does not seem to have entirely endeared himself to young Jago, as he tells us, again in 'Edge Hill':

> Hail, Solihull! respectful I salute
> Thy walls; more awful once, when from the sweets
> Of festive freedom and domestic ease
> With throbbing heart to the stern discipline
> Of pedagogue morose I had returned.

It is one of those curious coincidences that Samuel Johnson later applied for a teaching post under this same pedagogue, but was turned down. The governors were satisfied with his scholarship, but thought him haughty and ill-natured and were worried that his scruffy appearance and the way he kept 'distorting his face' might have had an adverse effect on his pupils.[12] They were right; Johnson was never a success as a teacher.

From Solihull they both went up to Oxford: Shenstone to Pembroke and Jago to University College, but while Shenstone was entered as a Commoner, Richard Jago, whose father could not afford to support him, was a Servitor, and so it was difficult for them to meet, let alone carry on their friendship, for, as Graves explains, 'it being then deemed a great disparagement for a commoner to appear in public with one on that situation'. But they did meet in private and they remained the closest of friends for the rest of their lives; indeed Shenstone's letters to Jago provide biographers with much of their source material. And Jago remembered him warmly in 'Edge Hill':

> Nor can the muse, while she these scenes surveys,
> Forget her Shenstone, in the youthful toil
> Associate; whose bright dawn of genius oft

---

[12]David Nokes, *Samuel Johnson* (London, 2009), p49

Smooth'd my incondite Verse; whose friendly voice,
Called me from giddy sports to follow him
Intent on better themes – called me to taste
The Charms of British song, the pictur'd page
Admire, or mark his imitative skill.

Shenstone's voice was not always so friendly when considering 'Edge Hill'. Writing to Jago in 1762 he said, '... I never considered it otherwise than as a Poem which it was very advisable for you to compleat and *finish*.'[13] Rather faint praise, and it is as well Jago did not live to read the introduction to an edition of his poems published in 1822 where a Mr Davenport spares him nothing:

> This kind of poem must, therefore, depend for its charm rather upon the tender, or solemn, or picturesque trains of ideas which it excites ... than on its rigid fidelity in the delineating of external forms. Of this principle Jago appears to have been either ignorant or careless. This fault often gives to his work the dryness of a topography or of book of the roads, clothed in rhyme.

But what Davenport failed to recognise is that the criteria he erects and then blames Jago for not meeting were never part of his scheme of things. He did not intend to write another 'Grongar Hill'. The poem is more varied than that. It does feature a good deal of landscape poetry, but as we have already seen, it also contains elements of autobiography, and encomia on his friends, added to which are narrative, philosophical and historical sections. It is admittedly, quite unremarkable for the most part and thumpingly Miltonic; however, in Book 3 there is something Davenport missed and for which Jago does deserve our attention.

We are used to landscape poems and their descriptions of meadows, vales and streams, but here he takes us into the industrial

---

[13]Letters, p645

midlands, to the factories that had grown up in Birmingham and Aston and describes for us the molten metal flowing into the moulds.

> These the smoking kiln consumes
> And to the furnace's impetuous rage
> Consigns the solid ore. In the fierce heat
> The pure dissolves, the dross remains behind.
> This push'd aside, the trickling metal flows
> Through secret valves along the channel'd floor
> Where in the mazy mould of figured sand.
> Anon it hardens. Now the busy forge
> Re-iterates its blows, to form the bar
> Large, massy, strong …

Here, in a poem published in 1767, we have a vivid and well-informed picture of the Industrial Revolution. In terms of poetry it is, one might almost say, revolutionary. Little more than twenty years separate this from Thomson's final corrections to 'The Seasons', and yet the notion of decorum which is so apparent there does not hold Jago back. After explaining the industrial process he goes on to tell us about the things – everyday things – that are made in these factories.

> How the coarse metal brightens into forms.
> What various use! See the glittering knife
> Of tempere'd edge! the scissors double shaft,
> ………………..     the button round,
> Plain or imboss'd, or bright with steely rays!
> Or oblong buckle on the lacker'd shoe
> With polish'd lustre bending elegant
> It's shapely rim. But who can count the forms
> That hourly from the glowing embers rise?

*Scissors* was not a word Alexander Pope was prepared to use, far too lacking in decorum. In *The Rape of the Lock*, admittedly a

mock-heroic, they had been 'the glitt'ring forfex'. With Jago we
are introduced to an altogether different England.

Jago's *Miscellanies* were given an equally blunt dismissal by Mr
Davenport and perhaps with more reason: 'They are, in general
such verses as many could write, and which few persons will read.'
He excepts 'Blackbirds' and 'Goldfinches', the poems for which
Jago was best known, as being works in which 'simplicity and
tenderness are united'. Simple they are, but sentimental and
bordering on the mawkish. In the first, the cock blackbird courts
his mate – for eleven stanzas – in the worst of contemporary fashion.

> O fairest of the feather'd train!
>    For whom I sing, for whom I burn
> Attend with pity to my strain,
>    And give my love a kind return.

She, seeming not to mind his hackneyed diction and over-worked
rhymes, returns his passion, but before they have a chance to live
happily ever after, 'A gunner met them in the vale.' The male bravely
sacrifices himself and 'the plumy maid' is spared. The elegy ends:

> Divided pair! forgive the wrong
>    While I with tears your fate rehearse,
> I'll join the widow's plaintive song
>    And save the Lover in my verse.

It is worth noting perhaps that such feeling for wildlife was not
common at this time; it is not a feeling which Jago's mentor William
Somervile would have shared. But Jago's knowledge of actual birds
seems to have been somewhat sketchy. The cock blackbird offers
to build a 'plaister'd nest', but it is the thrush not the blackbird
that lines its nest with mud. And he fares no better in his elegy on
goldfinches. The goldfinch is one of the tiniest British birds,
weighing no more than half an ounce, yet he suggests that 'the

ponderous stick' forms part of this tiny creature's nest! This nest is stolen by a truant schoolboy, the 'most ungentle of his tribe', leaving the pair to mourn in 'secret sadness'.

Mr Davenport was of the opinion that, 'Trifles, to have any merit, must at least be elegant ... The trifles of Jago have no claim to this praise.' And he was probably right, but while Jago was not a good poet, Shenstone's other close friend, Richard Graves, was, and which may be more to his credit, a good man too. Respected by his patron, Lord Willoughby de Broke, to the extent that he presented him with the lucrative living of Kimcote in Leicestershire, worth £400 a year and which proved to be a sinecure, as he chose to remain Vicar of Snitterfield, a parish only a few miles from where he had been born. And there he lived from 1754 until his death in 1804 at the age of 86, a tender parent, according to one obituary, a kind master, a hospitable neighbour and sincere friend, and a faithful, worthy minister of the parish over which he presided.

Much of what we know about William Shenstone's life depends, as has already been said, on the letters he wrote to Richard Jago. In addition, there is the extended biography by Richard Graves written as a series of letters under the title of *Recollections of some Particulars in the Life of the late William Shenstone Esq* and published in 1788. It is from these letters that we learn many of the particular personal details which could have been known only to a friend. But it is from *Collections for the History of Worcestershire,* compiled in 1781 by the antiquarian Treadway Russell Nash, that we find a touching story of Shenstone's childhood. He learned to read when very young, we are told, and had such a passion for books that whenever any of his family went to the market he begged them to bring him back a book, and if by chance they forgot, his mother would wrap a piece of wood up in paper and take it up to his bedroom where he would hug it to his pillow. A nice story, but what tears there must have been in the morning and how cheated he must have felt.

It is to Graves we owe the account of their meeting at Pembroke. When he first went up, Graves was part of a sober, water-drinking, Greek-reading group, but was 'seduced', as he put it, into joining a party of west-country lads who drank ale, smoked and sang songs. Then he moved up a rung socially and became part of a port-drinking society who regarded themselves as 'bucks of the first head'. Shenstone he encountered in both of the latter groups, but not among the water-drinkers. We are told that Shenstone's chief academic interests were mathematics, logic, natural and moral philosophy rather than poetry with which he only 'amused himself occasionally'. Graves goes on to tell us that his friend was somewhat bashful in society, but he must have been inwardly quite self-assured as, contrary to the fashion of the day, he wore his own hair and not a wig, which 'often exposed him to the ill-natured remarks of people who had not half his sense'.[14]

According to Graves, Shenstone was very attracted to academic life, but, as we have seen, life at The Leasowes proved to be even more attractive and he left Oxford without taking a degree. Graves, on the other hand, stayed on and was elected to a Fellowship of All Souls at the age of 21, which, even allowing for the more lax standards of the time, was a remarkable achievement. He did briefly consider and even took a few steps towards a career in medicine, but settled on the Church and was ordained in 1741. He held a curacy in Aldworth, twenty miles north of Oxford, but spent a good deal of time at his family home at Mickleton in Gloucestershire. Here he fell in love with Utrecia Smith, the

---

[14]Richard Graves, *Recollections*, p26

daughter of his first school master. By all accounts she was a very remarkable woman of 'outstanding learning and ingenuity'. Shenstone fell in love with her too, but it was Graves whom she favoured and there was a 'connection' of four or five years between them, but one which Graves confesses 'for prudential reasons, he thought better to break off'. Marriage would have meant an end to his fellowship. The poor girl died – some say of a broken heart, some say smallpox – shortly afterwards and was 'greatly lamented by Mr Shenstone, and many more ingenious young people'.[15] Graves must at least have felt some guilt about this as he was moved to raise a commemorative urn to her in Mickleton church. It is still there today. And Shenstone wrote his Elegy IV in her memory.

But Graves's prudence seems to have deserted him altogether during his curacy at Aldworth. There he took lodgings with Edward Bartholomew, a yeoman farmer with five daughters. Lucy, the youngest, was only fifteen, half Graves's age, and he fell in love again, but it was not her mind which attracted him this time. Lucy became pregnant. He did the honourable thing and married her, but secretly in The Fleet. Clearly he did not want news of it to reach the authorities at All Souls and probably not his immediate family either. They would not have been pleased and, significantly, there is no reference to them in any of his later correspondence. However, it is good to be able to record that the members of the Warwickshire Coterie seem to have taken her to their hearts. The social gulf between Richard and Lucy would have been likely to have caused a problem, but it was solved by the ingenious notion of sending her off to a London boarding school to acquire the graces she would come to have need of.

It would not look to have been the most promising start to a

[15]Letters, p.; 645[15]ibid, p115-116

marriage, but it proved to be one of lasting happiness and in Volume IV of Dodsley's anthology there is a moving little poem called 'The Parting', subtitled 'Written Some Years after Marriage', which contains the lines:

But oh! the fatal hour was come
    That forc'd me from my dear;
My Lucy then thro' grief was dumb,
    Or spoke but by a tear.

Now far from her and bliss I roam,
    All nature wears a change:
The azure sky seems wrapt in gloom,
    And every place looks strange.

The most curious thing about these two amorous adventures is that they both feature in Graves's satirical novel *The Spiritual Quixote* a picaresque work owing more to Fielding and Sterne than to Cervantes. Among its frequent digressions the story of Utrecia is told, with some Gothic elaboration, by a Mr Graham in Book IV, and that of Lucy – now called Charlotte Woodville – is recounted with warmth and tenderness and at length in Book VI by a Mr Rivers. Neither of these individuals play any other part in the overall story and it does look as though Graves may be looking back and giving voice to some feelings of guilt.

Later in the novel this *roman à clef* element is dropped when Mr Wildgoose, the satirised protagonist, a Methodist lay-preacher prone to disasters, finds himself in Halesowen where to his surprise he meets up with William Shenstone whom he had known at University.

... the Gentleman turned his face towards them, when Wildgoose immediately discovered him to be no other than his old acquaintance, the now celebrated Mr Shenstone, whose place began to be frequented by people of distinction from all parts of England, on account of its natural beauties, which, by the mere force of genius and good taste, Mr Shenstone had improved and exhibited to so much advantage. And this had discovered to the world his own fine poetical talents and polite learning, which, from his modesty, would otherwise probably have been buried in solitude and obscurity.

Wildgoose, as the story goes, inevitably causes another catastrophe: considering Shenstone to be too attached to worldly things he overturns his statues and destroys his cascades.

Shenstone had died in 1763, ten years before the publication of *The Spiritual Quixote*. He never married. His younger brother Joseph had died in 1751 and so, there being no immediate family, it was Richard Graves, along with Robert Dodsley, who undertook to act as his executor. In addition to the poems which Shenstone had been preparing for publication, there was a considerable amount of unpublished material, much of it in prose. The editing fell to Graves and in 1764 Dodsley published two handsome volumes of the verse and prose, followed the next year by a volume of the letters. Then in 1779 Graves brought out his novel *Columella* which was immediately looked on as being a portrait of his friend and finally in 1788 came his *Recollections of some Particulars in the Life of the late William Shenstone, Esq*, prompted by Johnson's less than generous treatment of him in his *Lives*.

Graves was in his 70s by this time, but his energy was certainly not failing him. Successful writer, meticulous editor, loving husband, caring parent and compassionate pastor, he was also a forward-thinking educationalist, running a small boarding school in Claverton where two of his pupils went on to achieve fame. One was Robert Malthus, the economist and author of the *Essay on the Principles of Population*. The other was Thomas Bowdler, who presented the world with his *Family Shakespeare*, an edition omitting out all of what he thought were the naughty bits, and in doing so, gave his name to any such silly editorial procedure.

It was in 1804, at the age of 89, that Richard Graves died peacefully, having outlived all the members of the Warwickshire Coterie: Somervile, Lady Luxborough, Shenstone, Jago and Whistler.

Anthony Whistler is the member of the coterie about whom we know least. Born in the same year as Shenstone, he was of somewhat higher social standing. His family held the lordship of the manor of Whitchurch near Pangbourne in Oxfordshire and Graves describes him as 'a young man of great delicacy and sentiment'.[16] He was educated at Eton, though educated might be putting it too strongly; as Graves adds, ' … though, with every assistance at Eton, he had such a dislike to learning languages, that he could not read the Classics in the original'. And as the Classics took up almost the entire curriculum at that time it is hard to see what kind of education he did acquire. Nevertheless he had a genuine love of literature and Graves concedes that 'no one formed a better judgement of them (the Classics)'.

He and Graves were invited by Shenstone to join him in his rooms at Pembroke in a kind of 'Breakfast Club' to which each was to bring with him a text for discussion. Whistler brought *The Rape of the Lock* and was later to produce a mock-heroic poem of his own, 'The Shuttlecock'. It ran to 39 pages, but vanity and wealth ensured that it was published in an elegant edition, tastefully bound in leather. The short poems which Dodsley published – at Shenstone's request – in Volume IV of his anthology are tedious enough.

Like Shenstone, Whistler also left the university without taking

---

[16]Ibid, p18

a degree; he did not intend to follow any sort of career. Despite their differences, the two men remained friends, but it was a friendship which flourished best at a distance and in their correspondence. When they met, the differences caused problems. After one visit in 1751 Shenstone wrote to Graves, 'I have never received a single line from Mr Whistler and I believe my journey to Whitchurch has given the final blow to our friendship.'[17] This is hardly surprising, as Shenstone had no time for two of the activities which were the mainstay of social life in such circles: cards and dancing. Graves put it very clearly:

> But to cards he always had a great aversion; and as for dancing … he used to express his contempt of that diversion, which he was incapable of enjoying. He used to say, it was allowable only in savages, and that in the rudest style, of jumping about, as an expression of joy. But for a set of people, capable of conversing rationally, to start up with an affectation of mirth, which they do not feel, and with *regulated* motions prance about the room, he said, it was like running mad by rule.[18]

Shenstone's visit coincided with Whistler's decision to invite two or three of the most respectable families in the neighbourhood for a ball and a supper. It did not bode well and proved to be anything but. Graves had described Whistler as having a 'delicacy of taste, and softness of manners, bordering on effeminacy' and this was not how Shenstone lived. As he told Graves,[19] 'I never was fond of that place. There is too much trivial elegance, too much punctilio for me.' If that was how he felt, perhaps he should not have gone, and as he did go he might have behaved better. Graves tells us exactly how the visit went:

---

[17]*Letters*, p319
[18]Graves, p41
[19]ibid, p149-151

'They do nothing but play at cards,' says he, 'and, on account of my ignorance of any creditable game, I was forced to lose my money, and, *two evenings* out of seven, at Pope Joan with Mr P — 's children.' This disposed him to ridicule Mr Whistler's great solicitude in preparing for his entertainment: instead, therefore, of paying any regard to the hints which were given him, that it was time to dress for their company, Mr Shenstone continued lolling at his ease, taking snuff and disputing rather perversely on the folly and absurdity of laying a stress upon such trifles, and, in short, the dispute ran so high, that, although Mr Shenstone suppressed his choler that evening, yet he curtailed his visit two or three days and took a cool leave the next morning and decamped.[20]

It is hard to see what reason Mr Shenstone had for his choler. His behaviour was boorish and Whistler showed some restraint in not writing to him.

But a year later they were friends again, and in 1754 Shenstone told Graves that 'If Mr Whistler would give me a visit in the height of my season this year, I should look upon it as one of the most pleasing events that could happen in the remainder of my life.'[21] That was in April. In June Whistler caught a cold, contracted a sore throat and died. Everyone was shocked by the suddenness of it. Shenstone wrote to Graves:

The melancholy account of our dear friend Whistler's death was conveyed to me, at the same instant, by yours and by his brother's letter. I have written to his brother this post; though I am very ill able to write upon the subject, and would willingly have waved it longer, but for decency. The triumvirate which was the greatest happiness, and the greatest pride, of my life is broken! The fabric of an ingenuous and disinterested friendship has lost a noble column! yet it may, and *will*, I trust, endure till one of us be laid as low.[22]

---

[20] *Letters*, p398
[21] ibid, p401
[22] ibid, p403

# 3

# THE POET

IN 1751, AFTER SHENSTONE HAD 'DECAMPED' from his friend Anthony Whistler's house in something of a huff, he headed for home, reaching the Sunrise Inn at Edgehill by evening, and there, Graves tells us,[1] he wrote down what was to become the closing stanza of a poem which appears in Volume V of Dodsley's anthology under the title 'Written at an inn on a particular Occasion':

> Whoe'er has travell'd life's dull round,
>     Wher'er his various tour has been,
> May sigh to think how oft he found
>     His warmest welcome – at an inn.

In Shenstone's *Collected Poems*, which Dodsley edited, it was included in the section headed 'Levities, or Pieces of Humour'. Samuel Johnson had dismissed all these pieces as 'exempted from the severities [and what a very telling word that is] of criticism' but adding nevertheless that their 'humour is sometimes gross, and

---

[1] Richard Graves, *Recollection of some Particulars in the Life of the late William Shenstone, Esq* (London, 1788), p152

seldom spritely'. This was, however, a stanza which he was able to recite from memory when he and Boswell were staying at the Swan Inn at Henley-on-Thames.

> 'No, Sir,' (he said); 'there is nothing which has yet been contrived by man, by which so much happiness is produced as by a good tavern or inn.' He then repeated, with great emotion, Shenstone's lines.[2]

It may have been this incident which led Dodsley, and subsequent editors, to give the poem the misleading title 'Lines written at an inn in Henley', when he later put together the *Collected Poems*, as Shenstone can have been nowhere near there, nor near Henley-in-Arden. Carelessly, Dodsley also missed out the fifth stanza and later editors have again followed him. In full the poem reads:

> To thee, fair Freedom! I retire,
>     From flattery, feasting, dice and din;
> Nor art thou found in domes much higher
>     Than the low cot, or humble inn.
>
> 'Tis here with boundless power I reign,
>     And every health which I begin,
> Converts dull port to bright champain;
>     For Freedom crowns it at an inn.
>
> I fly from pomp, I fly from plate,
>     I fly from Falsehood's specious grin;
> Freedom I love, and form I hate,
>     And chuse my lodgings at an inn.
>
> Here, waiter! take my sordid ore.
>     Which lacqueys else might hope to win;

---

[2]Samuel Johnson, *Lives of the English Poets* III, p358

It buys what courts have not in store,
  It buys me Freedom, at an inn.

And now once more I shape my way
  Thro' rain or shine, thro' thick or thin;
Secure to meet, at close of day,
  With kind reception – at an inn.

Whoe'er has travell'd life's dull round,
  Where'er his various tour has been,
May sigh to think how oft he found
  His warmest welcome – at an inn.

This is what was referred to in the eighteenth century as an occasional poem, but in this instance it is clearly a very specific occasion: Shenstone's flight from all the pomp and show, the form and fastidiousness which had irritated him so at Whistler's. We sense his irritation in that ragged second line with its biting alliteration, 'From flattery, feasting, dice and din'. And the artificiality of it all is succinctly captured in his picture of 'Falsehood's specious grin'. He simply had to get away from it all: the word 'Freedom' is there in each of the first four stanzas, and when we come to the end we can hear his sigh of settled contentment in those repeated, closing words: 'at an inn'.

It is not a poem for which one would wish to make exaggerated claims, but it is no surprise that Johnson remembered it. It is a poem which does exactly what it sets out to do and is in all respects very accomplished. It is a poem which, as Auden once put it:

> a man of
> honour, awaiting death from cancer or a firing squad,
>   could read without contempt.

(The Cave of Making)

If one were to sit down and read Shenstone's Levities one after the other, as I strongly suspect was the case with Dr Johnson, of course they would appear trivial, indeed inevitably and increasingly trivial as such poems were never meant to be read in this way. That should be obvious, but unfortunately it does not always appear to be so. Let us, in contrast, imagine a situation in which we are opening our morning's post and find, written out for us in longhand, a poem – one single poem – from our friend William Shenstone. It would be a delightful discovery, amusing and enjoyable. Undemanding but enjoyable. And one would never know what to expect: the Levities are so varied, both in subject and verse form. Added to which, Shenstone had a real talent for comic rhyme. In a poem about a rat that ate some books, we are told:

> In books of geo-graphy
> He made the maps to flutter;
>     A river or a sea
>     Was to him a dish of tea;
> And a kingdom, bread and butter.

And there are one or two such, I would contend, which still deserve to be read. 'Colemira' purports to be an eclogue, but an Horatian epigraph, 'Nec tantum Veneris, quantum studiosa culinæ' (pursuant not so much of love as of the kitchen), gives us due warning. These are not shepherds but skivvies working in a kitchen. Hence it is a 'Culinary Eclogue' and the commonplaces of low-life, and rather greasy commonplaces they sometimes are, come pushing their way up through an elegant veneer. The poem opens:

> Night's sable clouds had half the globe o'erspread,
> And silence reign'd, and folks were gone to bed.

Damon is lying by the fire among the cats and dogs and singing to them the praises of his beloved Colemira, a name which seems to combine both coal and mire. She is praised, as a damsel should be, for her 'goodly cheeks', yet ...

> But sure no chamber-damsel could compare,
> When in meridian lustre shines my fair,
> When warm'd with dinner's toil, in pearly rills
> Adown her goodly cheeks the sweat distils.

He praises too her 'mellow voice':

> When from the hearth she bade the pointers go,
> How soft, how easy, did her accents flow!
> 'Get out,' she cried.

Then gives the dogs a kick, which Damon tells us he would 'as lief I had the kick as they'. And so it continues, the bathos being handled quite splendidly. Undemanding, but nevertheless amusing.

'To a Friend' goes a step further and in doing so raises an interesting literary issue. Once again we are in a kitchen where Ned and Sal are playing cards. It is Sal's turn, but she cannot make up her mind which card to play, much to Ned's annoyance. The couplets catch the tone of the argument perfectly. Ned tells her:

> 'That card will do – blood never doubt it,
> It's not worth while to think about it.'

But she hesitates for so long that she plays the wrong card and loses.

The narrator, who is telling this story to his friend, observes:

> Methinks, old friend! 'tis wondrous true
> That verse is but a game at loo.

The issue is whether a poem should be a matter of a moment's thought or something carefully crafted. It is the issue which R.S. Thomas depicted in his early poem 'Poetry for Supper', where one bard insists that:

'Listen, now, verse should be as natural
As the small tuber that feeds on muck
And grows slowly from obtuse soil
To the white flower of immortal beauty.'

An argument which his friend rejects.

'Man, you must sweat
And rhyme your guts taut, if you'd build
Your verse a ladder.'

It is the age-old argument which Keats was in no doubt about,
telling John Taylor that 'If Poetry comes not as naturally as Leaves
to a tree, it had better not come at all.' Shenstone acknowledges
the ease with which his friend (probably Richard Jago) writes and
contrasts it with the 'strange heats' others indulge in:

Through fragrant scenes the trifler roves,
And hallow'd haunts that Phoebus loves:
Where with strange heats his bosom glows,
And mystic flames the god bestows.
You now none other flames require
Than a good blazing parlour fire;
Write verses – to defy the scorners
In shit-houses and chimney-corners.

Nothing quite prepares us for that last line.

Back at the card game, Sal dithers again and loses again and
Shenstone once more praises and celebrates his friend's skill, but
rather more decorously this time:

You, who can frame a tuneful song,
And hum it while you ride along,
And trotting on the king's highway
Snatch from the hedge a sprig of bay,
Accept this verse, howe'er it flows,
From one that is your friend in prose.

Shenstone's own method of working, one may deduce, was rather more laborious than his friend's, but his portrayal of the argument as a game of cards is quite as telling as that of Thomas or Keats: his tone relaxed, his thinking exact.

∗ ∗ ∗ ∗

Overall, Shenstone's verse came in for a good deal of adverse and at times even derisive criticism. Johnson, as one might expect, pulled no punches: ' ... his diction is often harsh, improper and affected; his words ill-coined or ill-chosen, and his phrase unskilfully inverted'.[3] Walpole called him 'that water-gruel bard'[4] and Gray excelled his own sarcastic self, ' ... he goes hopping along his own gravel-walks, and never deviates from the beaten path for fear of being lost'.[5] Hazlitt later described his poems as 'indifferent and tasteless'.[6] Even the more rational Donald Davie, in the introduction to his mid-twentieth century anthology *The Late Augustans*, said he was 'undoubtedly very small beer as a poet.'[7] Nevertheless, almost everyone regarded 'The School-Mistress' as an exception, even Gray who, in a letter to Walpole, called it 'excellent in its kind and masterly'.[8]

It is certainly a poem which Shenstone put time and effort into. Its first appearance was in his slim volume *Poems Upon Various Occasions* which has as a subtitle *Written for the Entertainment of the Author, and Printed for the Amusement of a few Friends, prejudiced in his Favour*. It was privately printed for him in Oxford

---

[3]ibid, p355
[4]Marjorie Williams, *William Shenstone* (London, 1935), p102
[5]Thomas Gray, D.C. Tovey ed (London, 1909) *The Letters* II, p25
[6]William Hazlitt, *Lectures on the English Poets* (London, 1830), p236
[7]Donald Davie, *The Late Augustans* (London, 1958) pxx
[8]Thomas Gray, *Letters*, I, p183

in 1737 during an extended stay at his old college. He was then 23. We do not know how his friends responded, but Shenstone himself, as we have seen, became so prejudiced against it that he was at pains to collect and destroy any copies he could lay his hands on. It is not easy to see why he did this. It is an attractive little book and while it does contain one or two stanzas he might have preferred not to own up to later, it also included, in addition to 'The School-Mistress', 'The Speeches of Sloth and Virtue', most of which was to reappear in his long poem *The Judgement of Hercules* (1741) And Robert Dodsley was happy, and rightly so, to publish 'Colemira' and 'Verses to a Lady' together with a number of the book's shorter poems in his 1764 *Collected Works*. But Shenstone's decision does show how seriously he was taking his poetry and his reputation.

'The School-Mistress' purports to be an imitation of Spenser; at least it adopts the Spenserian stanza and is an imitation of the way in which Spenser was regarded at the time. Writing to his friend Richard Jago in 1741 Shenstone said, ' ... there are some particulars in him that charm me: those which afford the greatest scope for ludicrous imitation are his simplicity and obsolete phrases'.[9] The 1737 version certainly does abound in obsolete phrases from the very beginning:

> In evrich Mart that stands on British Ground,
> In evrich Village less y-known to Fame,
> Dwells there, in Cot uncouth, a far renown'd
> A Matron old, whom we School-Mistress name;
> Who wont unruly Brats with Birch to tame:
> They grieven sore in Durance vile y-pent
> Aw'd by the Pow'r of uncontrouled Dame;
> And oft-times on Vagaries idly bent
> For Task unconn'd, or unkempt Hair are sore y-shent.

---

[9]Marjorie Williams, *The Letters of William Shenstone*, p36

And the narrative is a simple one, telling us of her use of the birch. One miscreant has been caught looking at the picture of St George on the back of his horn-book instead of the letters and words on the front. Despite his tears and protests at the injustice of it, he is beaten. Later her heart softens and she gives them all sugared cakes and gingerbread, but this 'Wight of Bum y-galled', still outraged, will have none of it and goes into a sulk. The other children then run out to play or go off to the Huxter's cottage, and the poem ends with two stanzas describing all the good things to eat which can be found there.

Most of what features in the 12 stanzas of this version re-appears, with some changes, in the later editions, but stanza nine does not.

> Algates the rest from silk Misfortune free,
> Stir'n but as Nature doth abroad them call;
> Then squatten down with Hand beneath each Knee,
> Ne seeken out or secret Nook or Wall,
> But Cack in open Street – no Shame doth them appal.
> And may no Carl their Innocence deride,
> While they piss as boldly, in the face of all;
>    Turning unaw'd their Vestments small aside,
>    Ne covet Hedge ne Barn their privy Parts to hide.

The call of nature is brilliantly depicted in this little vignette. Breughel might have painted it. The detail of 'Then squatten down with Hand beneath each Knee' shows a degree of observation which, had Shenstone been prepared to repeat, might have changed the direction of eighteenth-century poetry. But he did not. Readers of the time were not squeamish about such matters, as a glance into Pope's *Dunciad* will show, while among the brief notices at the back of a 1753 edition of the *Monthly Review* there is listed 'Bum-fodder: a Poem for Ladies on Soft paper', but looking back

Shenstone seems to have decided that his 23-year-old self had slightly over-stepped the bounds of decorum.

At this stage it is important to establish why Shenstone chose to depict his school-mistress in 'A Poem in imitation of Spenser's stile'. She was *his* school-mistress, as he told Jago. It was ' … a portrait of my old school-dame Sarah Lloyd whose house is to be seen as thou travellest towards the native home of thy faithful servant'.[10] He was very conscious that he was doing something for which there was no literary precedent; rustic realism was a far remove from the pastoral ideal. Sarah Lloyd was no youthful shepherdess; she was an old woman and quite clearly a woman of the lower social orders. In literary terms the lower orders were almost invariably regarded as figures of fun. We always need to remember that the first definition of 'Clown' in Johnson's dictionary is 'A rustick, a country fellow, a churl.' Our later use of the word as someone to be laughed at says it all. To deal sympathetically in verse with a person such as Sarah Lloyd therefore presented a problem. A mock-heroic might have been attempted. Pope had already set a precedent with his remarkable Spenserian poem 'The Alley' in which he had depicted the very low life which coagulated in London's dockside area:

> Her dugs were mark'd by every Collier's Hand.
> Her Mouth was black as Bull-Dogs at the Stall;
> She scratched, she bit, and spar'd ne Lace ne Band,
> And Bitch and Rogue her Answer was to all;
> Nay, e'en the Parts of Shame by Name would call:
> Yea when she passed by or Lane or Nook,
> Would greet the Man who turned him to the Wall,
> And by his Hand obscene the Porter took,
> Nor ever did askance like modest Virgin look.

---

[10]ibid, p46

But Shenstone did not want to go that far. Nevertheless, imitation was an accepted literary genre, so, by adopting the Spenserian stanza and archaic language he could be seen as basing something new on something which seemed to have a tradition behind it.

He had a genuine respect for Sarah Lloyd and was anxious lest people should look on the poem as being in some way silly or childish. He wrote to Graves, 'But if a person seriously calls this… a childish or low species of poetry, he says wrong.'[11] How then could he avoid being laughed at? One way to defray laughter was to invite it, but to do so on his own terms and so reduce it to a degree of affectionate warmth. To this end, in the second version, published separately by Dodsley in 1742, he told Graves that he had 'added … a ludicrous index purely to show (fools) that I am in jest'. For example, the stanza telling us of Sarah Lloyd's concern for her pet hen is designated in the index as 'A Digression concerning her Hen's presumptuous Behaviour, with a Circumstance tending to give the cautious Reader a more accurate Idea of the officious Diligence and Oeconomy of an old Woman.' His notion of a 'jest' seems to have differed somewhat from ours.

Priced at sixpence, it was an attractive little volume with engravings of designs done by Shenstone himself: the frontispiece being of the school house with the ominous birch tree growing alongside it, and as he described it to Jago, 'with the sun setting and gilding the scene'. It is a very different poem from his youthful performance, having 16 added stanzas, but he was still not satisfied and a third version appeared six years later in the first volume of Dodsley's *Collection of Poems by Several Hands.* Clearly he had gained in confidence. The archaisms are fewer; the defensive burlesque of the index and the portentous footnotes are dropped,

[11]ibid, p48

and another seven stanzas have been added. As an epigraph it now has a pair of wry lines from Virgil's vision of Hades which translate as 'straight away are heard voices and a great wailing and the weeping souls of infants on the first threshold of sweet life'. And below is an 'Advertisement' which points in a new direction.

> What Particulars in SPENSER were imagin'd
> most proper for the Author's Imitation on this
> Occasion, are, his Language, his Simplicity, his
> manner of Description, and a peculiar Tender-
> ness of Sentiment, visible throughout his Works.

It is the 'peculiar Tenderness' which is significant as in this final form we have a nostalgic and generously warm-hearted poem.

Putting its readers at their ease, it opens on a familiar note: a little didactic platitude declaring that it regrets 'To think how modest worth neglected lies' and that it will 'sound the praise of merit'.

Sarah Lloyd's merit is presented to us in terms of how she lives ' … in lowly shed and mean attire'. None of that dreaded word 'luxury' here, and this is stressed again in Stanza 6:

> Her cap far whiter than the driven snow,
> Emblem right meet of decency does yield;
> Her apron, dyed in grain, as blue, I trowe,
> As is the hare-bell that adorns the field.

There is a charming neatness and delicacy in that comparison with the hare-bell. But she is no softy either. She wields the 'Tway birch sprays', as was to be expected of a teacher then, and what chaos there would have been, Shenstone insists, if she had not – no 'comely peace of mind and decent order'. Her pupils are rightly in awe of her:

> For they in gaping wonderment abound,
> And think, no doubt, she been the greatest wight on ground.

These lines may have lingered in Goldsmith's mind: the pupils at his school in Auburn looked at their teacher and were amazed 'That one small head could carry all he knew.'

One of the additions Shenstone made to his original picture of her is that of her pet hen which she lavished such care on and which it in its turn lavished on its chicks. It all helps to persuade us of her merit, as it is this hen, we are told, which is 'the plodding pattern of the busy dame'.

This is followed by three stanzas listing the herbs which grew in her garden, but it is not simply a list, as Shenstone, a herbalist himself it would seem, points out their several uses:

> And Plantain ribb'd, that heals the reaper's wound;
> And Marj'ram sweet, in shepherd's posie found;
> And Lavender, whose spikes of azure bloom
> Shall be, ere-while, in arid bundles bound,
> To lurk amidst the labours of her loom,
> And crown her kerchiefs clean, with mickle rare perfume.

On Sundays she sings the Psalms as translated by Sternhold and Hopkins and teaches her pupils about the terrible tortures inflicted by 'papal rage', with Shenstone adding as an aside:

> Ah! dearest Lord, forfend, thilk days should e'er return.

Nothing of this nature was voiced in that first version, but here in stanza 17 he reverts to what had been its stanza 3: the discipline and the story of the little lad caught failing to pay proper attention. Now we have it in detail.

> Ah luckless he …
> For brandishing the rod she doth begin
> To loose the brogues, the stripling's late delight!
> And down they drop; appears his dainty skin,
> Fair as the furry coat of whiten Ermilin.

And in an added scene his little sister bursts into tears at what is about to happen and almost rushes out to defend him. But the punishment is given and the others wisely settle down to their work, while he 'bum y-galled' is left to cry. The realism of such a homely scene is far ahead of its time.

It is the injustice which the little boy finds so hard to take, and when Sarah Lloyd offers them all compensating gingerbread, he refuses.

> And still the more to pleasure him she's bent,
> The more doth he, perverse, her haviour past resent.

And goes off into his splendid sulk.

At this point Shenstone issues a warning to village school teachers not to quell the spirits of their charges, as: 'nurs'd with skill, what dazzling fruits appear'. He suggests that among them might be a future bishop, a chancellor in embryo, or a 'bard sublime ... as Milton' and this, it should be noted, two years before Gray published his Elegy with its 'village Hampden' and 'mute inglorious Milton'.

As the poem comes to a close he returns to the scene (minus the lavatorial element) he had first painted in 1732: the children running out to play, to sing or just saunter about, or going down to the lake to play at ducks and drakes. There is such freshness in the detail here. He has no qualms about mentioning such things in verse. Many of his contemporaries would not have dared. Even Thomson could not have brought it off; his Miltonics would not have allowed it.

Surprisingly he makes very few changes in the final three stanzas which are a bright and succulent list of all the fruits which the children could have spent their pennies on at the nearby huxter's cottage. The final page of the 1742 edition shows Shenstone's drawing of a tempting heap of such things: grapes and plums, a melon and a Catherine pear, but it seems that even without that illustration he still could not bring himself to 'murder his darlings'. They are fine stanzas with some memorably luscious lines, but it is hard to see how they constitute an ending to a poem about a school-mistress. Indeed Sarah Lloyd seems to have been quite forgotten; there is no mention of her in the nine preceding stanzas, and the close is a celebration of Shrewsbury cakes and of their maker! It is nevertheless a fine poem in many respects and a brave one. Shenstone had undertaken something quite new and, in doing so, he paved the way for Goldsmith's 'The Deserted Village' and for Wordsworth's 'The Old Cumberland Beggar', a poem which many readers still found shockingly ungenteel more than half a century after Shenstone had celebrated 'A Matron old whom we School-mistress call'.

In 1741, the year before the second appearance of 'The School-mistress', Dodsley had published *The Judgement of Hercules*, in a form which differs considerably from that in *The Works* of 1764. It tells of the choice which Hercules, in his youth, had been obliged to make between Pleasure and Virtue. We know which one he chose, so the 'debate' – here the contestants are named as Ease and Fame – is never in doubt, and besides, in his 'Essay on Elegy', Shenstone had made it clear that in his view, 'The most important end of all poetry is to encourage virtue.' The presentation of the two also shows that there is really no contest. Virtue steps forward 'in artless folds of white', while Pleasure is a bit of a gaudy slut, all wiles and 'tinsel beauty'.

It is a long poem in heroic couplets with little to commend it. Of course Hercules chooses Fame and Virtue and is eager to face up to its hazards and hardships, but it is interesting that at the time of writing Shenstone had just inherited The Leasowes and must have been considering his own future. We know that he rejected the city for a life of rustic contentment, and in the poem one cannot help feeling that the sensuous snares of Ease as they are presented to us have far more attraction about them than the onerous challenges of Fame. I am not at all convinced that Shenstone is not secretly on her side. Time and again Graves would later accuse him of indolence. The poem seems to have been a success, however, as Graves tells us that 'Mr Shenstone had the satisfaction, at a coffee-house, to hear the judicious remarks of some young people on his poem; who came to a resolution, that, it must certainly be either Pope's or Mr R. Dodsley's.'[12]

Between 1737 and 1746 Shenstone wrote 19 Songs. Dodsley, in his Preface to *The Works* (1764) remembered 'a passage in one of his letters where, speaking of his love songs, he says, "The reason there are so many, is that I wanted to write ONE good song, and could never please myself".'[13] An explanation which is a far remove from Walpole's sarcastic recollection of it twenty years later, when he suggested that Shenstone kept at it because he '… was labouring through his whole life to write a perfect song, and in my opinion at least, never once succeeded.'[14] An unkind remark, but it has to be said that there is some truth in it. Many of the songs are so bland as to have slipped the reader's mind even before the last line is reached. The themes are ever the same: lovelorn shepherds, Damons and Daphnes beset by nightingales and nymphs.

> Ye shepherds! give ear to my lay,
> And take no more heed of my sheep;
> They have nothing to do but to stray,
> I have nothing to do but to weep.

---

[12]Graves, p93
[13]Shenstone, *Works*, I, p11
[14]Williams, p102

In certain respects the pastoral/rococo was at the height of its popularity at this time and it was not only Marie Antoinette and her friends who were dressing up as rustics to play in the Petit Trianon, so was Bolingbroke at his 'farm' at Dawley. It provided a recurrent setting for many of the new Italian operas and Fragonard and Watteau were at work on paintings which still appeal today. But pastoral poetry of the eighteenth century is not taken seriously. Dr Johnson had no time for it at all. His essay on the subject in *Rambler* 38 concludes:

> The facility of treating actions or events in the pastoral style, has incited many writers, from whom more judgement might have been expected, to put the sorrow or the joy which the occasion required into the mouth of Daphne or of Thyrsis, and as one absurdity must naturally be expected to make way for another, they have written with an utter disregard of both of life and nature, and have filled their productions with mythological allusions, with incredible fictions, and with sentiments which neither passion nor reason could have dictated.

And we tend to agree with him; yet we should recognise that Shenstone was trying to do something different. Turning his back on the didacticism and high seriousness of the heroic couplet and all that Pope represented, he was looking to bring back the lyric, something with feeling and emotion, something with delicacy and grace, something which could be set, as were the poems of Elizabethan days, to music. And in this his four-part sequence 'A Pastoral Ballad' achieved some success, being set to music by one of the most distinguished composers of the time, Thomas Arne. Indeed Arne wrote to Shenstone to tell him that 'Any Song, Cantata or Dramatic Piece, from so delicate a Pen ... would be the most welcome present I could receive.'[15]

---

[15]ibid, 104

Despite its jaunty anapaests and its conventional tone, there is something about 'A Pastoral Ballad' which suggests that it perhaps recounts a case of unrequited love in Shenstone's own life. What is unusual and surprising about it is that the opening stanza of the first part *Absence* has as its final line 'I have left my dear Phillis behind.' Now in such cases it is always the Phillis who goes off and leaves her lover disconsolate. Here it is the lover who does the leaving. Why? He does not seem to know himself.

> But why do I languish in vain?
> Why wander thus pensively here?
> Oh! why did I come from the plain,
> Where I fed on the smiles of my dear?

But in his *Recollections* Richard Graves is in no doubt and tells us of Shenstone's stay in Cheltenham in 1743. It had, apparently, been his passion for Graves's sister, two years earlier, which had prompted Shenstone to sketch out his 'Pastoral Ballad', but in Cheltenham, 'becoming very intimate with Miss C—, who is still living, he became so far enamoured, as to feel himself unhappy on leaving Cheltenham and the object of his passion. On this occasion he enlarged, and divided it into the four distinct parts under the titles of *Absence, Hope, Solicitude* and *Disappointment*.'[16] With this in mind, when we approach Part 2, Hope, with our eyes and ears open, it is soon evident that the picture he is painting for us is not the archetypal Rossa/Lorrain landscape of so much pastoral poetry, but something far more localised and individual. Indeed it must be The Leasowes:

> My banks they are furnish'd with bees,
> Whose murmur invites one to sleep;

[16]Graves, p104

> My grottos are shaded with trees,
> And my hills are white over with sheep.
> I seldom have met with a loss,
> Such health do my fountains bestow;
> My fountains all border'd with moss,
> Where the harebells and violets grow.

And everything he does there, he tells us, is in the hope that she will fall in love with the place and with him:

> One would think she might like to retire
> To the bower I have labour'd to rear:
> Not a shrub that I heard her admire,
> But I hasted and planted it there.

She has, it would seem, visited him there and in stanza five we perhaps hear a conversation they have had:

> I have found out a gift for my fair;
> I have found where the wood-pigeons breed;
> But let me that plunder forbear,
> She will say 'twas a barbarous deed:
> For he ne'er could be true, she averr'd
> Who could rob a poor bird of its young ;
> And I loved her the more when I heard
> Such tenderness fall from her tongue.

But, sadly, it comes to nothing. She loves another and, it seems, belongs to a higher social status than Shenstone:

> Beware how you loiter in vain
> Amid nymphs of a higher degree;
> It is not for me to explain
> How fair and how fickle they be.

Again, Graves confirms this, and though Johnson would have it that 'he might have obtained the lady, whoever she was, to whom his Pastoral Ballad was addressed',[17] his friend knew differently:

But, indeed, I hardly can believe, as her sister was married to a baronet of considerable fortune, that Miss C— [her name was Carter] in her bloom, would have condescended to marry a man, however deserving, of so small a fortune as Mr Shenstone. And though, from his acquired habits and taste of life, he could not have been happy with a woman of inferior education, yet as he was sensible his income was not sufficient to support a lady of Miss C— 's description, he never aspired to that happiness.

He was disappointed, as the title of Part 4 tells us, but he determined to be happy with The Leasowes:

Yet time may diminish the pain:
The flower, and the shrub, and the tree
Which I rear'd for her pleasure in vain,
In time may have comfort for me.

And also, we may assume, with writing poems such as 'A Pastoral Ballad', which even Johnson found reason to praise: 'In the first part are two passages, to which if any mind denies its sympathy, it has no acquaintance with love or nature.'[18] It was a poem which Dodsley was eager to include in his anthology, but it was constantly passing to and from among Shenstone's friends, especially Lady Loughborough, and he seems never to have felt quite satisfied with it; the result being that it was not published until the posthumous *Works*. As he once wrote to Lady Loughborough, 'I am well aware that my Pegasus is one of those dull Horses which will not bear to be hurry'd. Allow him but his time, and he may jog on safely, but urge him to move faster, and he is sure to break one's neck.'[19] The frustration Dodsley felt at this is there in his letters, from which we learn just how careful, not to say pernickety, Shenstone could be:

[17](opposite page)Johnson, III, p353
[18]Ibid, p356
[19]*Letters,* p359

God grant me patience! But you cannot be in earnest? What, rob me of the most beautiful piece in the collection when I have boasted of it to everybody? Why should you alone insist upon that absolute perfection to which no human production did ever yet arrive?[20]

It was the same, as we have seen, with Shenstone's *Songs* and while we may not want to read all of them, we should at least recognise what he was seeking to do. We should remember too that Robert Burns, who had a practical appreciation of these things, was a keen admirer of Shenstone, which is not surprising when we read ballads such as 'Slender's Ghost', in which he identifies with poor Abraham Slender of 'The Merry Wives of Windsor', who, even long after his death, still tenderly harbours memories of 'O sweet! O sweet Anne Page!' The poems of Shenstone which Burns was particularly fond of, however, were the Elegies. He wrote that they 'do honour to our language, our nation, and our species',[21] and Shenstone himself would seem to have regarded them as being among his most significant pieces as his *Collected Works* opens with 'A Prefatory Essay on Elegy'. In it he immediately endears himself to the reader with a wryly ironic opening gambit. Prologues, he confesses, 'are contrived very frequently to inculcate such tenets as may exhibit the performances to the greatest advantage' (and he had not had the advantage of reading Mr Wordsworth). What follows, however, is a reasoned and balanced account. True to the classical traditions of his day, he notes that there are 'few rules given us by the critics concerning the structure of elegiac poetry' (all quotations from the Essay are as they appear in *Collected Works* of 1764) but goes on to provide his readers – if not with rules – with some critical observations of his own. Granting the wide variety

---

[20]Robert Dodsley, *The Correspondence*, ed. James Tierney (Cambridge, 1988), p332
[21]Williams, p105

of subjects and the many different styles to be found in elegies, he asserts that 'in its true and genuine acceptance' an elegy should include 'a tender and querulous idea'. Here he is using the word in what Johnson gives as its first meaning: 'mourning' – there is no implication of peevishness. They are ideas which he then re-states in a nicely telling metaphor: 'It throws its melancholy stole over pretty different objects; which, like the dresses at a funeral procession, gives them all a kind of solemn and uniform appearance.'

Historically, he suggests, elegy began by commemorating the death of friends and relatives and of illustrious men, but, exhausting this theme went on to express grief at 'absent or neglected lovers' and from there to all aspects of love until it covered 'any kind of subject, treated in such a manner as to diffuse a pleasing melancholy'.

A man of his time, he then moves on to consider the purpose of elegy and declares, 'the most important end of all poetry is to encourage virtue'. Epic and tragedy, he tells us, 'recommend the public virtues' while elegy 'endears the private'. There are, he says, 'sweets in melancholy which we could not find in mirth'.

Virtue, we are not surprised to be told, will always be found in the innocence and simplicity of rural life, but in this respect elegy differs from pastoral, having an elegance and refinement which raise it above 'unpolished rusticity'. Not that his 'Pastoral Ballad' had much 'rusticity' about it and we know how much polishing it underwent.

Opposed to the celebration of wealth and power which he finds in much of the poetry of his day, he envisages elegy 'encouraging the sweets of liberty and independence ... the honest delights of love and friendship' and the celebration of 'the glory of a good name'.

Turning to a consideration of style, his prime concern is for simplicity and as for versification, although he recognizes the strength of Pope's couplets, he finds them too restrictive, while poems such as 'Lycidas' have too much freedom with their rhymes being so far apart as hardly to be discernible. For a degree of discipline, yet coupled with an element of flexibility, it is the ten syllable quatrain which he advocates.

Again, the classicist in him prompts his defence of the use of English or modern allusions, and he hopes that such will not be imputed to his ignorance, but there is a new note to be heard in his assertion that these elegies are personal statements occasioned 'as particular incidents in life suggested' and that in his rural scenes he 'drew his picture from the spot'. He concludes with a return to the solidly Augustan belief that 'poetry without morality is but the blossom of a fruit tree', but there is something so very fresh about the metaphor he chooses to express it.

The opening poem in Shenstone's *Elegies Written on Many Different Occasions* can be viewed as a re-statement in verse form of many of the observations in the 'Prefatory Essay'. Its full title is 'He arrives at his retirement in the country, and takes occasion to expatiate in praise of simplicity.' It is written in quatrains, the form he had advocated and which he credited to James Hammond, who had published his 'Love Elegies' in 1743. Hammond had merited a few pages in Johnson's *Lives*, but was brusquely dismissed: 'He produces nothing but frigid pedantry' and Johnson went on to wonder 'Why Hammond or other writers have thought the quatrain of ten syllables elegiac it is difficult to tell.'[22]

Shenstone's 'Elegy' begins by stating that he has left the city and its 'venal sins' to live where 'rural virtues' may be found. He

---

[22]Johnson, II p315

expresses his scorn for poets who celebrate power and wealth in order to attract some of it to themselves:

> Still may the mourner, lavish of his tears
> For lucre's venal need, invite my scorn!
> Still may the bard, dissembling doubts and fears,
> For praise, for flattery sighing, sigh forlorn! (17-20)

Above all, what he wants to see in verse, he says, is simplicity:

> O loved Simplicity! be thine the prize!
> Assiduous Art correct her page in vain. (13-14)

Yet in using words such as *assiduous* he is hardly following his own advice.

And then in lines which have echoed down through the years from Sidney's assertion in 'Astrophel and Stella', 'Look in thy heart and write', he stresses the need for personal sincerity:

> Write from thy bosom – let not art control
> The ready pen that makes his edicts known. (31-32)

It is a poem which, as can be seen, has the makings of a literary manifesto. Shenstone was not an amateur, one of the gentlemen 'who wrote with ease'. But did he reach his full potential? Dodsley thought not. In his Preface to the *Collected Works*, he again accuses him of indolence, telling us that 'he chose rather to amuse himself at the foot of the mount, than to take the trouble of climbing the more arduous slopes of Parnassus'.[23] Dodsley knew him well and was an experienced and astute editor, so we must take seriously what he says, and yet the wide variety of topics Shenstone approached in the pages which follow shows that he was constantly in search of something new, something different. There are poems

---

[23]Shenstone, *Works*, I pv

which are openly didactic, and poems mourning the death of friends. In addition, there are narrative poems, love poems and several which are keenly concerned with contemporary political and social issues, and others of a truly personal nature recounting events in his own life and that of his friends.

Number IV, 'Ophelia's Urn', refers to the early death of Utrecia Smith, that remarkable young woman whom Shenstone and Graves were both in love with, and to whom Graves – perhaps out of guilt – had erected a commemorative urn in Mickleton church. In Graves's opinion this was 'the most correct'[24] of all the elegies and one of his favourites, but the correctness is perhaps part of the problem. We have no reason to doubt the strength of feeling behind the poem, but the surface is smothered under the conventions of the Gothic graveyard scene and cluttered with the coldest of personifications:

Then young Simplicity, averse to feign,
Shall, unmolested, breathe her softest sigh,
And Candour with unwonted warmth complain,
And Innocence indulge a wailful cry.                    (25-28)

Even so, and again this is sometime prior to the publication of Grays's more famous 'Elegy', we find him able to end a stanza with 'Why, like the desert's lily, bloom'd to fade?'

The didactic element predicted in the Preface is, as one would expect, to be found throughout the sequence: pastoral, in whatever form it takes, being inherently a critique of urban society. In its celebration of rural simplicity and advocating a retreat from the court and the city, it stands in opposition to the materialistic values and corruption which are presumed to be endemic there.

All this and more features in another of the elegies singled out

---

[24]Graves, p117

by Graves, Number VI, 'He Describes his Vision to an Acquaintance'. It opens with a graveyard scene again, but presented to us this time with a good deal more conviction. In his dream he is in Suffolk, wandering along the banks of the River Orwell, near the birthplace of Thomas Wolsey. It is a starless, autumn night, a storm is brewing and he is alone:

> Then the dull bell had given a pleasing sound;
> The village cur 'twere transport then to hear;
> In dreadful silence all was hush'd around
> While the rude storm alone distress'd mine ear. (7-10)

The phantom which, inevitably, appears to him is the Cardinal himself in full scarlet regalia, but there is nothing frightening about him; indeed he instantly offers his help:

> 'Stranger,' he said, 'amid this peeling rain,
> Benighted, lonesome, whither wouldst thou stray?
> Does wealth, or power, thy weary step constrain?
> Reveal thy wish, and let me point the way.' (21-24)

And he goes on to explain just what power he once had and to boast, not unreasonably, of his achievements:

> 'Low at my feet the suppliant peer I saw;
> I saw proud empires my decision wait;
> My will was duty, and my word was law,
> My smile was transport, and my frown was fate.' (33-36)

This of course not only allows the dreamer to reject any such offer, but to lecture the ghost on the folly and perils of ambition. To achieve it, he asks:

> Must I not groan beneath a guilty load –
> Praise him I scorn, and him I love betray?
> Does not felonious Envy bar the road?
> Or Falsehood's treacherous foot beset the way? (61-64)

The ghost, as we might expect, has no answer to any of this:

> And, sighing, vanished in the shades of night.              (80)

There is rather more narrative skill evident in these Elegies than one might expect from a poet in the middle years of the eighteenth century. 'Elegy XXVI' recounts the confession of a young rake, telling of how he had seduced Jessy, a naïve village girl, and then given her money so she could sail away from her shame, and how her ship was wrecked on the high seas and she and her child both drowned. Curiously, this Elegy is singled out for special praise by Ruskin in that most bizarre and cold-blooded piece of literary criticism, his thoughts on the 'Pathetic Fallacy', which he describes as being, 'always the sign of a morbid state of mind and comparatively of a weak one'. By way of contrast he cites, 'Two most exquisite instances from master hands.' One is the story of the ruined maid Ellen in Wordsworth's 'The Excursion'. The other is Shenstone's similar story of the seduced and deserted Jessy. He quotes the lines

> If through the garden's flowery tribes I stray,
>     Where bloom the jasmines that could once allure
> 'Hope not to find delight in us,' they say,
>     For we are spotless, Jessy; we are pure.'

To our astonishment he then adds, 'The perfection [of this passage] as far as truth and tenderness of imagination … is quite insuperable.' Yet there is still a caveat. 'Jessy is weaker than Ellen, exactly in so far as something appears to her in nature which is not. The flowers do not really reproach her. God meant them to comfort her, not to taunt her; they would do so if she saw them rightly.' These are pronouncements which tell us far more about Ruskin, I would suggest, than they do about Shenstone, yet it is

interesting to see that he is still being read more than a hundred
years after his death, even by someone as seemingly hostile to
poetry as John Ruskin.[25]

Equally remarkable is 'Elegy XVI', narrating what seems to be
an actual event, that of a deranged young woman wandering about
on Salisbury Plain seeking her divine (literally divine, such is her
derangement) lover. Such tales come as a surprise to us; it would
be more than half a century before Wordsworth's female vagrants
and mad mothers were to be seen as introducing a new era into
English poetry, while at the same time puzzling and perplexing his
first readers.

Some of the social and political issues Shenstone tackled were of
only passing interest: a proposed tax on luxury items and a
momentary blip in the British woollen industry. But others were
among the gravest of his time: slavery and body-snatching. He was
prepared to accuse western slave-owners of hypocrisy in their claim
to be Christian. He has a slave speak out:

> 'Of blissful haunts they tell, and brighter climes,
> Where gentle maids, convey'd by Death, repair,
> But stain'd with blood, and crimson'd o'er with crimes,
> Say, shall they merit what they paint so fair?'  (XX 53-56)

It took courage to confront such matters in verse; unfortunately
he lacked the courage to break free from the Augustan reliance on
tradition, believing that it was still possible to write about them in
terms of the pastoral. In his book on pastoral Terry Gifford wrote
that 'pastoral is a discourse, a way of using language that constructs
a different kind of world from that of realism'.[26] But when the
realism is as vile as slavery and body-snatching, then the language

[25]Ruskin, *Selected Writings* (Oxford, 2004), p79
[26]Terry Gifford, *Pastoral* (London, 1999), p45

of the pastoral strikes us as wholly inappropriate. In 'Elegy XXII', Sylvia, a young woman who has died overseas and whose body has been returned to lie with her parents, begs that her grave be protected from the Resurrection-Men and her body from the anatomists. She does not want her remains

> gash'd beneath the daring steel,
> To crowds a spectre, and to dogs a prey.                    (65-68)

Powerfully put, but when it is Damon of whom she is begging help, we cannot but wonder whether it is really fair to expect that of a shepherd.

When Shenstone does step out from under the shadow of the pastoral we hear a very different voice: more at ease with itself, more assured. And we hear it most clearly in 'Elegy XI', 'He Complains how Soon the Pleasing Novelty of Life is Over'. It is dedicated and addressed to Richard Jago and the opening line has a delightfully relaxed and colloquial tone:

> Ah me, my Friend! it will not, will not last

The topic is nothing new and stanza 2 seems to be following the familiar *ubi sunt* theme:

> Where are the splendid forms, the rich perfume?
> Where the gay tapers, where the spacious dome?
> Vanish'd the costly pearls, the crimson plumes,
> And we, delightless, left to wander home!

But it is nicely handled with variations in the position of the caesura and the heavy, falling sound of that tellingly banal last line. But these generalities quickly give way to the actualities of his own life. They are his own disappointments and failures he is lamenting. He had, he tells us, hoped for some worldly and social success, 'On the world's stage, I wish'd some sprightly part.' He had wanted to be a painter, then a poet, but it had all come to nothing. He even dismisses as a failure his landscape gardening:

> Oft too, I pray'd: 'twas Nature form'd the Prayer,
> To grace my native scenes, my rural home;
> To see my trees express their planter's care,
> And gay, on Attic models raise my dome.          (29-32)

He returns to the tradition, saying how it had all looked so rosey in the days of his youth, but it had been a delusion. Time has so dulled his senses that even nature offers no balm:

> Tedious again to curse the drizzling day!
> Again to trace the wintry tracks of snow !
> Or, soothed by vernal airs, again survey
> The self-same hawthorns bud, and cowslips blow!
>
> O Life! how soon of every bliss forlorn!
> We start false joys, and urge the devious race;
> A tender prey; that cheers our youthful morn,
> Then sinks untimely, and defrauds the chase.          (53-60)

The personal elements, while clearly there, are not developed in any detail. The time was not right for poetry of an outright personal nature. Pope's autobiographical statements are presented as imitations of Horace. Shenstone shows some signs of recognising a possible change in direction – a direction in which other poets such as Smart and Collins and, a little later, Cowper, were taking a few hesitant steps. But none had the vision to see that it was possible to write 'The Prelude' and even here we have to remember that while Wordsworth wrote it in his early days, it was not released for publication until after his death.

However, when we pause to look back and consider Shenstone's aims and ambitions and take stock of his achievements, we begin to realise that his poems amount to rather more than Davie's 'very small beer'.[27] It is evident from his letters that he greatly admired both Pope and Thomson, but he wanted to free himself from the heroic couplet and from blank verse. Instead he wrote songs and lyrics, and ballads in which he showed he could imagine himself into situations and feelings other than his own. In 'The School-mistress' he wrote with warmth and understanding of humble people and in its different versions we can observe a move towards greater simplicity of language. And in his Elegies he wrote from his own personal experience and of places he knew. Simplicity, imagination and subjectivity: an interesting agenda.

Shenstone knew his own worth and was saddened by his lack of recognition. In Elegy X, 'To Fortune', he protests that it does not bother him:

> Guiltless of Envy, why should I repine
> That his rude voice, his grating reed's preferred.        (47-48)

But overall it sounds as though he doth protest too much. But fame can often be no more than a matter of chance. It so chanced that Charles Darwin was first credited with the formulation of ideas which had long been circulating in the minds of others. Shenstone, it could be contended, was quietly but consciously among the pioneers if not at the actual forefront of the great changes which were then taking place in eighteenth-century literature. The chance did not come his way and it was not in his nature to go hunting for it.

---

[27]Davie, p*xi*

# 4

# THE ESSAYIST

THE REVEREND GEORGE GILFILLAN, IN THE Preface to his edition of Shenstone's *Poetical Works* (1854), observed rather tartly that 'few volumes of poems contain less thought than his'. There may be something in this, but it could be argued that thought is not necessarily what we first look for in a poem. Robert Dodsley, writing in 1764, came close to sharing Gilfillan's opinion in his own Preface to the *Collected Works*, but added ' ... his character as a man of clear judgment and deep penetration will best appear in his prose works'. And here Dodsley may well have been right. In these essays, *Men and Manners*, we learn so much about the ideas, the values and tastes of his time, and especially where landscape gardening is concerned. Added to which Shenstone shows himself not only to have been an astute observer of human nature, but one with a sense of humour. We instantly recognise the truth of his remark that 'The most reserved of men, that will not exchange two syllables together in an English coffee-house, should they meet at Ispahan, would drink sherbet and eat a mess of rice together.' And, as is so evident here, an additional strength is that of his prose

style. It has little of the Johnsonian rhetoric and *balance* which can
become rather tiresomely pompous after a while. Discursive, almost
at times to the point of diffusiveness, his tone is so relaxed that
some of these pieces come to us with all the qualities of good
conversation and with a common sense which belies their wisdom,
a wisdom, what's more, which is coupled with compassion, a quality
not frequently met with in the middle years of the eighteenth
century.

The opening essay, 'On Publications', begins by adopting an
amusingly self-deprecatory stance:

> 'Tis not unamusing to consider the several apologies that people
> make when they commence authors. It is taken for granted that, on
> every publication, there is at least a seeming violation of modesty; a
> presumption, on the writer's side, that he is able to instruct or to
> entertain the world; which implies a supposition that he can
> communicate, what they cannot draw from their own reflections.

And then he adds, as a warning:

> When self-interest inclines a man to print, he should consider that
> the purchaser expects a penny-worth for his penny: and has reasons
> to asperse his honesty if he finds himself deceived. Also, that it is
> possible to publish a book of no value, which is too frequently the
> product of such mercenary people.

Such assertions are doubly relevant when we realise that
Shenstone himself did not publish any of these pieces in his own
lifetime; Dodsley appears to have found them among his papers
and collected them together after his death. It does not seem that
Shenstone circulated them among his friends either, as he did his
poems, for there is no reference to them in any of his letters.

Modesty is a quality he extols in one of his essays, while 'On
Vanity' begins:

Falsehoods upon a tomb or monument may be intitled to some excuse in the affection, the gratitude, and piety of surviving friends. Even grief itself disposes us to magnify the virtues of a relation, as visible objects also appear larger through tears.

It is not a profound statement. One might say that it 'oft was thought', and even if it can hardly be argued that it was 'ne'er so well express'd', the expression is, nevertheless, neatly put and memorable. Shenstone is not what one would call a thinker, but he was certainly a man of ideas, ideas which he presents to us like so many small impromptu epiphanies. But in truth, it becomes clear that far from being impromptu, each has been worked on, shaped, formed and honed down into that curiously un-English prose form, the aphorism. Once read, who is likely to forget 'The world may be divided into people that read, people that write, people that think, and fox-hunters'? Or again, 'Many persons, when exalted, assume an insolent humility, who behaved before with an insolent haughtiness.'

In a remarkable book, *The World in a Phrase – a Brief History of the Aphorism,* James Geary tells us that the aphorism is not only the world's shortest form of literature, but possibly its oldest, citing Lao-tu, Buddha and Confucius as being among its earliest exponents. It could even be said to go back to the *Chinese Book of Changes,* the *I Ching,* written some 5,000 years ago.

An aphorism, Geary tells us, is not the same as an adage, an epigram, a motto, or a proverb, and gives us five laws which an aphorism must meet:

It must be brief
It must be definitive
It must be personal
It must have a twist.
It must be philosophical

The last law, having been put forward by Friedrich Schlegal, who said that an aphorism contained 'the greatest quantity of thought in the smallest space'.[1] Geary's other 'laws' he justifies on the grounds that an aphorism is not a bland generalisation, but a deeply personal statement which asserts rather than argues, proclaims rather than persuades and which achieves maximum impact through paradox.

There have been famous aphorists. We have the bitterness and cynicism of La Rochefoucauld, the challenging assertions of Nietzsche and those vatic pronouncements of Wittgenstein: 'Uttering a word is like striking a note on the keyboard of the imagination.' But listing these names makes us aware that there is no Englishman to put alongside them. There is Alexander Pope, the brilliancy of whose wit and acumen has meant that many of his lines have dwindled into proverbs: 'To err is human; to forgive divine', but they are not and never were aphorisms, having always been part of a wider entity. Dictionaries of quotations devote page after page to the sayings of Samuel Johnson, but that verbal torrent was recorded by Boswell, not written by the doctor.

W.H. Auden was, characteristically, interesting, bombastic and quite probably right when he wrote in the Foreword to his *Faber Book of Aphorisms*:

> Aphorisms are essentially an aristocratic genre of writing. The aphorist does not argue or explain, he asserts, and implicit in his assertion is a conviction that he is wiser or more intelligent than his readers. For this reason, the aphorist who adopts a folksy style with 'democratic' diction and grammar is a cowardly and insufferable hypocrite.[2]

---

[1] James Geary, *The World in a Phrase* (London, 2006), p18
[2] W.H. Auden, *The Faber Book of Aphorisms* (London, 1964), pv

Of course, Auden is not suggesting here that the writers of aphorisms were all aristocrats (though many were) but that in their chosen form of writing they display that kind of poise and self-confidence which is not to be argued with. Now this may go some way to explaining why Shenstone did not publish any of his prose work. He knew the strength of his own ability – his letters provide ample proof of that – but his retiring nature meant that he was never one to call attention to himself, or push himself forward, even though he knew the cost: 'I am afraid humility to genius is as an extinguisher to a candle.' He wanted people to think he was special, but did not want them to think that he thought he was! The self-confidence is certainly there, however, and never more so than in his very worrying assertion that 'Every good poet includes a critic; the reverse will not hold.'

Another significant point that Auden makes is that:

> Two statements may be equally true, but, in any society at any given point in history, one of them is probably more important than the other, and, human nature being what it is, the most important truths are likely to be those which that society at that time least wants to hear.

And here too, Shenstone shows that he was by no means always seeking to amuse:

> 'If anyone's curse can effect damnation, it is not that of the pope, but that of the poor.'

From their very nature, aphorisms are not something one could read for more than a short length of time. The flicker-factor would soon have a hypnotic and eventually soporific effect, but as we dip into Shenstone's collection, certain ideas, attitudes and areas of interest do begin to call attention to themselves and tell us something about the man. He is, we gather, a kindly man, one who is, in many respects, untypical of what we have come to expect, rightly or wrongly, from men of his time. What we notice, as has already been said, is his compassion, even towards animals. We remember that his dog Lucy is by his side in Alcock's portrait of him. His opposition to fox-hunting was certainly not typical, but his concern for animals went so far beyond blood-sports as even to include insects: 'One should not destroy an insect, one should not quarrel with a dog, without a reason sufficient to vindicate one through all the courts of morality.' And this was many years before Blake was insisting that 'A Robin Redbreast in a Cage/Puts all Heaven in a Rage.'

Shenstone's concern for the poor was not confined to pious words either. At one time he was happy to allow entrance to anyone who wanted to visit The Leasowes, but it got out of hand. Some people picked the flowers and damaged his shrubs; his solution was to put up a warning, in verse, 'for the admonition,' as he told Jago, 'of my good friends the vulgar; of whom I have multitudes every Sunday evening, and who very fortunately believe in fairies and are no judges of poetry.' It began by claiming that fairies did actually live there:

> Here in cool grot, and mossy cell,
> We tripping fawns and fairies dwell.

His visitors should therefore be very careful:

> Then fear to spoil these sacred bow'rs;
> Nor wound the shrubs, nor crop the flow'rs;

For if they did:

> ill-betide or nymph or swain,
> Who dares these hallow'd haunts profane.

He was being optimistic of course in thinking that those who did believe in fairies were able to read.[3] Eventually he had to close his gates and be more selective in whom he allowed in. Those so favoured, however, were not always the wealthy. Dr Alexander Carlyle wrote in his autobiography about a visit to The Leasowes:

> I met with what struck me most – that was an emaciated, pale young woman, evidently in the last stages of consumption … with a little girl of nine or ten years old, who had led her there. Shenstone went up, and stood for some time conversing with her, till we went to the end of the walk and returned; on some of us taking an interest in her appearance, he said she was a sickly neighbour, to whom he had lent a key to his walks, as she delighted in them, though now not able to use it much.[4]

Another to whom Shenstone not only gave a key to his garden, but free access to his library was James Woodhouse, a local shoemaker. As a young man of 24, Woodhouse sent a poem to Shenstone which so impressed him that he took a personal interest in him ever after and greatly encouraged his career as a poet.

Servants seem to have given Shenstone some problems. He confessed that he had 'been formerly so silly as to hope that every servant I had might be made a friend', but found out that 'the nature of servitude is to discard all generous motives of obedience; & to point out no other than those scoundrel ones of interest and fear'. And on another occasion he wrote:

> The trouble occasioned by want of a servant, is so much less than the plague of a bad one, as it is less painful to clean a pair of shoes than undergo an excess of anger.[5]

But while a manservant could, at least briefly, be dispensed with,

---

[3]Marjorie Williams, *Letters of William Shenstone*, p202-203
[4]Marjorie Williams, *William Shenstone*, p54
[5]William Shenstone, *Works*, Vol II, p279

a housekeeper was an essential and, in Mary Arnold, Shenstone had a treasure. Even according to his pernickety friend, Anthony Whistler, she was, 'an Example of the simple force of moral Beauty',[6] but whatever he might have meant by that, she was far more, for she was practicality itself and nursed and fussed over her master during his many bouts of ill-health.

Also looking after him was a much younger and very different woman, Mary Cutler, for whom, it is suggested, his compassion contained more than a soupçon of actual passion. To understand her, there is something to be said for starting her story at the end. In 1768, five years after Shenstone's death, Catherine Hutton, the daughter of the Birmingham historian William Hutton, wrote in her journal of a visit she had paid with her mother to Ivey Farm, a house once belonging to Shenstone and in which Mary Cutler was then living with the aged Mrs Arnold. There she saw 'Shenstone's picture in oil, as large as life, and in a handsome frame.' On the back of it she was shown the words:

> This portrait belongs to Mary Cutler, given to her by her master William Shenstone Jan 1st 1754, in acknowledgement of her native genius, her magnanimity, her tenderness and fidelity.[7]

The words are in Shenstone's handwriting. E. Monro Purkis is very quick (altogether too quick in my view) to assure us that 'there is nothing in this, however, to show more than ordinary appreciation of a servant'. Really? *Magnanimity*? We may understand it as *generosity*, but Johnson's first definition is 'Greatness of mind'. And *tenderness*, he says, is 'Susceptibility to the softer passions', adding in support a quotation from Addison:

[6]Thomas Hull, ed. *Select Letters between the Late Duchess of Somerset, William Shenstone and Others* (London, 1778) Vol II, p30
[7]Audrey Duggan, *The World of William Shenstone*, p36

With what a graceful tenderness he loves!
And breathes the softest, the sincerest vows.

The ordinary appreciation of a servant? Hardly. Here we have Mary Cutler, who, Catherine Hutton observed, 'idolised the memory of her master', living out her retirement years in one of his houses; she has a portrait (it is the one by Ross) of him on her wall, and, according to report, possesses most of his books. And in the Wellesley College Library there is a small octavo notebook containing several water-colours of The Leasowes painted by Shenstone together with poems written out by him. On its hand-painted title page it states that he gave the notebook to Mary Cutler on January 1st 1754. This was no ordinary housemaid and she was clearly not regarded as such by Shenstone's friends either. Dodsley must have had a high regard for her: he sent her a signed copy of his play *Cleone* in 1758, and the year before that he had sent 'To my good friend Miss Mary a small canister of tea' as a Christmas present. And tea was not a cheap commodity in those days. The price of an average blend could be as high as ten shillings a pound, so was not the customary drink of servants.

We know very little about Mary Cutler, but what we do know is so very tantalising. She was evidently a cultured and intelligent woman, but she also seems to have been of some independent means. Leastways her financial situation is a puzzle. For several years – certainly from 1744 to 1749 – she received no wages at all. Shenstone must have been very short of funds as not only did he not pay her, he even borrowed money from her! It was in 1749 that she threatened to leave. He persuaded her to stay by offering to double her wages to £10 a year, but his promises do not look to have changed their financial relationship as when he died he owed her £500, which was a vast sum of money then and almost twice his own annual income. In his will he left her an annuity of £30 plus an extra £24 for looking after Mrs Arnold. But Mary Cutler had been made other promises: the settling of his debts to her and the tenancy of Ivey Farm. His executors contested this, but Mary seems to have had contacts and grit as well as money, as she took Richard Graves to the Chancery Court and won her case.

What was the relationship between Mary Cutler and her master? I think we can say she was his mistress. In Graves's novel *Columella*, the hero (who is in some respects Shenstone) seems rather depressed and his friends put it down to his home life. One tells him outright:

> 'Atticus and I have both agreed, that no servant would take the freedom which your house-keeper does with you, my friend, if you had not taken some freedoms with her.'[8]

Columella admits the truth of the situation and tells them, 'I have actually given her a contract of marriage; and yet I wouldn't marry her for the Indies.' Asked why, he says he cannot abide 'her rustic dialect'. His friend nevertheless advises him to keep his word. 'for I have generally observed more ill effects from violating than from pursuing such engagements'.

Richard Graves, as has already been noted, had himself married a farmer's daughter and lived happily ever after, so he would not have been opposed to Shenstone marrying his maid, but an irregular arrangement might have been something he could not approve of, and sometime later in the novel another friend observes:

> I should not mention it if the whole neighbourhood did not speak so freely of Columella's imprudence in this respect; in short, it is the improper connection with his house-keeper, which I believe he makes no secret of, or at least which he takes no care to conceal

---

[8]Richard Graves, *Columella* (London, 1779) Vol II, p74

from his other domestics, nor indeed from me. For whenever I have gone thither of late, she has always made the tea, and appeared as mistress of the house; which indeed is the reason that I could not in decency go thither as a visitor any longer.[9]

Graves might have looked approvingly on Shenstone marrying Mary Cutler, but what of Lady Luxborough? It is unlikely that she would have viewed it in the same way and friendship with her was something Shenstone would not have been prepared to put at risk. It is perhaps significant that while there are references to Mrs Arnold in his letters, there is no mention whatsoever of Miss Cutler. We will never know his feelings on the matter, for, as he advocated in one of his aphorisms, 'Prudent men should lock up their motives, giving only their intimates the key.' In this case, even his intimates seem to have been quite firmly shut out.

There can be little doubt that in most respects Shenstone was a good man, a virtuous man. He had declared in his essay on elegies that 'The most important end of all poetry is to encourage virtue.' He does not, however, seem to have been what one would call a religious man. The aphorisms and brief paragraphs which come under the heading of *On Religion* give no evidence of any religious commitment. There are, as one would expect, harsh words about the Pope and the Church of Rome, but the section opens with a somewhat agnostic tone: 'Perhaps, we should not pray to God "to keep us steadfast in any faith" but conditionally, that it be a right one.' What soon becomes clear is that Shenstone had no belief in absolutes:

When misfortunes happen to such as dissent from us in matters of religion, we call them judgments: when to those of our own sect, we call them trials: when to persons neither way distinguished, we are

---

content to impute them to the settled course of things.[10]

Rather a cynical attitude, but no less true for that, and the use of the term *our own sect* is telling in itself. It is a belief which he extends to warfare and the claims made by the victorious who offer up their thanks to God and assert that their success was due 'to the peculiar favour of a just Providence!' A protestation, he suggests, 'which argues more of presumption than gratitude'.

He extends this mistrust of absolutes into the field of ethics too. Just as there are people whose notions of beauty contradict ours, so, he says, there are societies whose members are happy to leave their parents behind them to be eaten by wild beasts, who will offer up human sacrifices to their deities, and who see nothing amiss in killing and then eating their enemies. This being the case, he suggests, 'there should seem to be no universal moral sense, and of consequence, none'. All this is a very far remove from the optimism of Pope's *Essay on Man*:

> In Faith and Hope the World will disagree,
> But all Mankind's concern is Charity.                    (IV 307-8)

Surely the outstanding entry in this section, however, reads: 'It is not now, "We have seen his star in the east" but "We have seen the star on his breast, and are come to worship him."'

The trappings which went with high office did not impress Shenstone in anyway, nor did titles, which he regarded as 'not so much the reward, as the substitutes of merit'. Opposed as he was to the personal display of luxury and extravagance, much has been made of him 'wearing his own hair' rather than a wig as fashion then demanded, but while he wrote of dress that 'Simplicity can scarce be carried too far,' he added, 'provided it be not so singular

---

[10]*Works*, Vol II, p298

as to excite a degree of ridicule'.[11] And there is nothing singular about the dark blue coat and buff-coloured waistcoat he wore for the portrait painted of him by Edward Alcock in 1760. It is very much of the time.

Simplicity was, for Shenstone, a watchword in so many areas of life. 'Dress,' he tells us, 'like writing, should never appear the effort of too much study or application.' Simplicity is a word we encounter time and again in his essay on elegies and is what appears to be behind his quarrel with Alexander Pope in the section headed 'On Writing and Books'. It was not that he questioned Pope's ability. Who could? But it seemed to him that he had ruled the literary scene long enough and that a change was needed, and it is in terms of ruling that he puts it:

> Let us not deny to Mr Pope the praises which a person enamoured of poetry would bestow on one that excelled in it: But let us consider Parnassus rather as a republic than a monarchy, where, although some may be in possession of a more cultivated spot, yet others may possess land as fruitful, upon cultivation.[12]

What he acknowledges is Pope's brilliance of economy, his 'consolidating or condensing sentences', but what he hesitates over is the excess of regularity and lack of imagination. And, not surprisingly, he twice expresses this concern in terms of landscape and gardening:

> Perfect characters in a poem make but little better figures than regular hills, perpendicular trees, uniform rocks, and level sheets of water, in the formation of a landskip. The reason is they are not natural, and moreover want variety.[13]

---

[11]ibid, p166
[12]ibid, p13
[13]ibid, p184

> I hate a style, as I do a garden, that is wholly flat and regular; that slides along like an eel, and never rises to what one can call an inequality.[14]

One of the longest and most interesting pieces in Shenstone's *Men and Manners* is, as one would expect, his 'Unconnected Thoughts on Gardening' and this will be looked at closely in a subsequent chapter, but the link he saw between poetry and landscape gardening is apparent in an early statement which could be taken as a reference to Pope's couplets as well as to an avenue of trees:

> It is not easy to account for the fondness of former times for straight-lined avenues to their houses: straight-lines walks through their woods; and, in short, every kind of straight line; where the foot is to travel over what the eye has seen before.[15]

Whereas Shenstone's aphorisms are by far the most noteworthy feature of *Men and Manners*, he does in fact set out his ideas for us in an interesting variety of prose forms. There are pen portraits and narratives as well as openly didactic statements, added to which there are times when he adopts another persona to voice his views and on one occasion puts contrasting ideas into the mouths of several contestants so that there is a brief dramatic debate. Dodsley may well have been right when he claimed that Shenstone's ideas 'best appear in his prose works'. There is certainly enough in them to contradict one of Shenstone's own assertions, namely that: 'A poet hurts himself by writing prose; as a racehorse hurts his motions by condescending to draw in a team.'[16]

---

[14]ibid, p176
[15]ibid, p130
[16]ibid, p189

# 5

# THE EDITOR

BOSWELL ONCE PUT IT TO SAMUEL Johnson that someone really ought to write a life of Robert Dodsley, but nothing came of his suggestion, which is surprising as he had lived such a extraordinary life. Born in Mansfield in 1704, the son of an impecunious schoolmaster, he received only the most basic of educations at his father's free grammar school, leaving there as soon as he was 14 to be apprenticed to a local stocking-weaver. Wisely, he absconded before his term was up and went off to London where he became a footman, an unlikely and inauspicious start for a man who was to become one of the most important and influential publishers of the century. Innate ability and a powerful business sense – and he clearly had both – would not have been enough to effect such a transformation in the prevailing social climate; he needed to have luck too, and Dodsley did very often find himself in just the right place at the right time.

His first master was Charles Dartineuf, reputedly an illegitimate son of Charles II. Dartineuf was a member of the Kit Cat Club, around whose dining table, therefore, would have been gathered such men as Addison, Steele, and Congreve as well as Lord Cobham and Sir Robert Walpole, listening to whom would, for footman Dodsley, have been something of a liberal education in itself.

More advantageous still was his subsequent move to London and into the household of the Honourable Mrs Jane Lowther, daughter of Viscount Lonsdale. She was a lady with a passion for literature and was delighted to discover that her new employee wrote poetry. This was when Stephen Duck, the Wiltshire thresher-poet, was not only attracting a growing audience, but royal patronage, so a London-based footman-bard had obvious market potential. She granted him free use of her library, and when his collection *A Muse in Livery* was published in 1732 she had secured a subscription list replete with the names of dukes and duchesses, counts and countesses and innumerable honourables. With so many members of the English nobility supporting the work of a footman, the book could not help but be an instant success, a success which emboldened Dodsley enough to leave domestic service and learn the trade of book-selling. He joined Pope's publisher, Lawton Gilliver, working under the appropriate sign of Homer's Head, where he learned all aspects of his new trade: the different sorts of paper and ink, typesetting, engraving, binding, advertising and selling, so that by 1735 he was able to open his own shop, financed by a gift of £100 from Alexander Pope himself. Pope had been pleased and impressed by a poem Dodsley had written in praise of him, but his generosity was not entirely selfless. One would not expect it to be. Having publishers indebted to him meant that he could ensure his works were produced exactly as he wanted them to be. He also had allies who would assist in the chicanery which went into the 'anonymous' printing of his letters.[1]

---

[1] For a full account of this see Maynard Mack *Alexander Pope: A Life*, pp653-672

From then on Dodsley was frequently referred to as 'Pope's publisher', but his interests and his achievements grew evermore wide-ranging. As well as publishing most of the minor classics of eighteenth-century poetry such as John Dyer's 'The Fleece', his imprint was also on many of the major ones, including Gray's 'Elegy'.

In 1738, when a poet no one had ever heard of offered him a manuscript which a number of other publishers had already turned down, he was able to see what they had missed and so gave the world 'London' by Samuel Johnson. And eight years later he was astute enough to recognise that this same poet and essayist was just the man he was looking for to compile a dictionary; a decision which had more far-reaching consequences than even he could have imagined.

Dodsley's shop at Tully's Head became the meeting place for the literati of the day, where young writers were to be seen and wanted to be seen, so it must have been with some trepidation that the reclusive William Shenstone, at the suggestion of Sir George Lyttleton, approached him with his poem *The Judgment of Hercules*. But the two men found that they had more than an interest in books and poetry in common. As an associate of Alexander Pope, Dodsley had paid many a visit to him at Twickenham, where he had seen the changes being made to his garden there, and of course landscape gardening was an area in which Shenstone was the expert.

Their friendship got off to a rather bumpy start though. 'The Judgment of Hercules' was well received when Dodsley published it in 1741. The following year he published an attractive edition of 'The School Mistress', but in 1748 there was trouble when he included it in the first volume of his collection *Poems by Several Hands*. He had not even asked permission and Shenstone made his displeasure quite clear in a letter to Richard Jago:

Dodsley has published my name to the School-mistress. I was a good deal displeased at his publishing that poem without my knowledge, when he had so many opportunities of giving me some previous information; but, as he would probably disregard my resentment, I chose to stifle it, and wrote to him directly upon the receipt of yours, that I would be glad to furnish him with an improved copy of the School-mistress, & for his second edition.[2]

He could have had no complaint about the company he was keeping in that volume as it featured Johnson's 'London', John Dyer's 'Grongar Hill', several poems by Lady Mary Wortley Montagu, and Collins's 'Ode to Evening'. The real trouble was that he no longer liked that earlier version and had been re-working it for some time. Dodsley agreed to replace the old with the new in the second edition, but that edition was already scheduled so he needed the copy right away. Speed of any kind was something quite foreign to Shenstone's nature and he drove Dodsley to distraction, but eventually all was well and the extended version as we now know it was published.

It is impossible to underestimate the importance and achievement of Dodsley's collection. When the final volume appeared in 1758 the *Monthly Review* declared that 'a more excellent Miscellany is not to be met with in any language',[3] an assertion which no one has since sought to challenge. One might say that there is something democratic about the choices made by this ex-footman. Only in half a dozen pages at the start of Volume III do we find the established figures of Pope and Thomson. Its emphasis is instead on the contemporary scene. Opening Volume I with the polished couplets of Thomas Tickell and closing Volume VI with the exuberance of Thomas Gray's 'The Bard', it traces and

[2]Marjorie Williams, *Letters of William Shenstone*, p133-134
[3]ibid, p487

embodies the progress of poetry during those middle years of the eighteenth century and did so for a nationwide audience, few of whom outside London were likely to have seen those first limited printings of poems such as *The Vanity of Human Wishes* and the *Elegy Written in a Country Churchyard*. It was through Dodsley's selection that these poems became known, as those six volumes were soon to be found on the bookshelves of every cultured person in the country.

There is nothing in any of the six volumes to suggest that the selection and editing were anything other than the work of Dodsley alone, but the correspondence which passed between the two men shows just how much he relied on the assistance, taste and judgement of Shenstone. Dodsley had written to him in September 1753, 'I am thinking of putting forward my Fourth Volume of Poems to Press, and should esteem it as a particular Obligation if you will contribute to render more acceptable to the Public, by favouring me with anything which you should think proper to appear in it.'[4]

Shenstone took the task put upon him very seriously, as again is clear from their correspondence, but there were times when his enthusiasm waned. Writing to Jago on 20 June 1755, he complains, 'I was obliged to devote my attention to the affair which I had so foolishly involved myself with Dodsley. You are unable to conceive what vexation it has given me.'[5] But there was vexation on both sides. Shenstone was, to put it mildly, pernickety, and manuscripts featuring the most minor of changes were constantly being interchanged among the friends as though there were no such things as deadlines. Shenstone was not to be hurried. He once confessed

---

[4]Dodsley's *Correspondence*, p156
[5]Wlliams, *Letters of William Shenstone*, p423

to Lady Luxborough, 'I am well aware that my Pegasus is one of those dull Horses which will not bear to be hurry'd. Allow him but his Time, and he may jog along safely; but urge him to move faster, and he is sure to break one's neck.'[6]

Eventually, however, the fourth volume was published, and the closing forty pages of it featured poems by every member of 'the Coterie': Somervile, Whistler, Jago, Graves and Shenstone, the final poem being his 'Pastoral Ballad', which is followed by a page of music composed especially for it by Thomas Arne.

Shenstone was delighted by the volume, praising Dodsley 'not only for the Pains you have taken, but for the Discernment you have shown'.[7] And he must have been even more delighted when the *Monthly Review* singled out 'Mr Shenstone's elegant and truly poetical pieces.'[8]

Then, in April 1756, at the end of one of his letters and making it look almost as an afterthought, Dodsley wrote, 'I certainly intend to publish two concluding Volumes to my Miscellany next winter if I can get materials sufficient, and such as are to my mind; in which I hope for your assistance.'[9] Perhaps he had forgotten his earlier frustrations, but if so, he was soon to be reminded of them.

Shenstone, it seems, would not stop making revisions and even revising the revisions. In letter after letter we sense Dodsley's growing impatience and sometimes it overflows:

> What is become of your Ode on Rural Elegance? I was in hopes to have seen it before this time: but I suppose it must now for some Months suffer a severe and causeless Persecution under your hands, for faults which nobody but yourself could accuse it of.[10]

---

[6]ibid, p359
[7]ibid, p.435
[8]ibid, p487
[9]Dodsley, *The Correspondence*, p2223
[10]ibid, p201

Shenstone had no business sense. Why should he? But Dodsley drove the point home that these delays were costing him money:

> I have between 6 and 7 hundred pounds bury'd in the Paper and print of this Edition, which I want to pay and cannot till I publish.[11]

Delays were not all that Dodsley had to cope with. Shenstone had earlier sent him the poem we now know as 'Elegy XXVI' but at that time it was simply referred to as 'Jessy'. With no warning, Shenstone declared he did not want to include it. Dodsley exploded.

> God grant me patience! But you cannot be in earnest! What, rob me of the most beautiful piece in the collection! What I have boasted of to everybody, shewn to several, and what all have admir'd. Dr Akenside says it is the most charming Elegy in any Language. I beg, my dear Sir, You will not think of depriving me of so valuable a treasure.[12]

But his pleas made no difference. Shenstone, for what reason we do not know, did not change his mind and it was not published until the posthumous volume of 1764.

Difficult though Shenstone may have been to work with, Dodsley – who had published most of the finest poets of that time – ever held him in the highest esteem, and it was to him he turned when looking for someone to write an 'Epilogue' to his play *Cleone*. The play itself has a very mixed history. Dodsley had first offered it to Garrick, then at the height of his career, but he had turned it down, calling it 'a cruel, bloody and unnatural, play'.[13] The subsequent fall-out between them was such that it became the talk of the coffee-houses. 'Doddy and Garrick have had a spat,' said Johnson[14] It was

---

[11]ibid, p334
[12]ibid, p332
[13]Marjorie Williams, *William Shenstone*, p80
[14]Duggan, op cit, p110

a spat that went so far as Dodsley even being forcibly turned away from Garrick's theatre one evening. But the play was eventually staged by John Rich at Covent Garden on 2 December 1758 and was a great success.

Shenstone's Epilogue to it had an equally varied history. He had seen the script as early as the summer of 1756 and had suggested some slight changes. It was then that Dodsley asked him to write an Epilogue. At that time Shenstone was still dragging his heels over contributions to the *Miscellany* and turned to Richard Graves for help, 'should any lucky hint occur to you'.[15] As we can see from a letter Graves wrote to Dodsley shortly after,[16] most of the groundwork was in fact his, but Shenstone's was the more prestigious name and it was finally attributed to him. As usual, however, it had passed to and fro between all three of them and as we learn from a letter Shenstone sent to Graves after the performance:

> Dodsley first liked, then disliked it, and lastly liked it again; only desiring me to soften the satire, shorten the whole (for it was upward of sixty lines), and add a complimentary close to the boxes. All this I have endeavoured, and sent it to him last Monday.[17]

Interestingly, the letter is dated 25 November, less than two weeks before the opening night; Shenstone was again leaving things to the very last moment.

While the Epilogue itself is in no way remarkable, its rhymed couplets are nicely modulated, with just enough enjambment and everyday diction to bring out the sound of a spontaneous speaking voice. It begins:

---

[15]*Letters*, p455
[16]Dodsley, p252
[17]*Letters*, p495

Well Ladies – so much for the tragic style –
And now the custom is to make you smile.
To make us smile! – methinks I hear you say –
Why, who can help it, at so strange a play?
The captain gone three years! – and then to blame
The faultless conduct of his virtuous dame!
My stars! What gentle belle would think it treason,
When thus provoked, to give the brute some reason?
Out of my house! – this night, forsooth, depart!
A modern wife had said – 'With all my heart –
But think not, haughty Sir, I'll go alone;
Order your coach – conduct me safe to Town –
Give me my jewels, wardrobe, and my maid –
And pray take care my pin-money be paid.

It is witty, relevant and encourages a positive response from the audience: all in all a skilfully crafted piece of work which Dodsley must have been well pleased with.

Shenstone and Dodsley had by this time become the closest of friends and as their letters show, they had, since 1751, been spending several weeks together every summer at The Leasowes. and in the summer of 1758 we find Dodsley again asking for a helping hand, this time with a proposed collection of fables.

There was a market for fables in the middle years of the eighteenth century as Dodsley, being a publisher, well knew. It could be said to have begun in 1727 with John Gay's collection which so caught the public imagination that it went into edition after edition. Others followed, among them Samuel Richardson and Christopher Smart. Smart, who translated Phaedrus, also wrote some twenty of his own. They did not appear in book form until after his death, but had proved so popular in his lifetime that they appear and re-appear in all the leading literary journals. And then there was Edward Moore's *Fables for the Female Sex*, tastelessly vacillating between the patronising and the openly chauvinistic. There was certainly a market and Dodsley's business sense detected a new niche in it.

In October 1758 he wrote to Shenstone:

> ...to let you into a secret, which is, that I am at present now writing from Aesop and others, an hundred select Fables in prose, for the use of schools; we having no book of that kind fit to put into the hands of youth, from the wretched manner in which they are written.[18]

Shenstone was hesitant at first, but when Dodsley arrived at The Leasowes the following summer, they were soon working amicably again together. At one stage he felt anxious about the project, writing to Graves, 'I wish to God it may sell, for he has been at great expense about it.'[19] But his worries were unnecessary. It was handsomely produced by Baskerville in Birmingham and hailed by the *Monthly Review:*

> We have now before us a very ingenious, a very elegant, and what is of still greater importance, a very useful work. It is indeed, in our opinion, a classical performance, both in regard to the elegant simplicity of the style and the propriety of sentiments and characters.[20]

Inevitably it is a volume which has disappeared down the maw of literary history, but one summer a visitor arrived who did have a lasting effect and he was Thomas Percy, a young man who would go on to compile his *Reliques of English Poetry*, a collection of ballads, which, one may say without exaggeration, was to lead to a revolutionary change in English poetry. But like all revolutions, it can be seen in retrospect to have had a slow and gradual build-up.

---

[18]Dodsley, p375
[19]*Letters*, p572
[20]Harry S. Solomon, *The Rise of Robert Dodsley* (Illinois, 1996) p34

That ballads come under the heading of verse few would dispute, but whether they merit being classed as poetry is an altogether different question and one not altogether unrelated to snobbery. A major factor which sets them apart is that ballads were, first and foremost, intended to be sung, added to which it seems certain that their first composers/singers never wrote their words down. Such compositions are folk-art, part of an oral tradition, which was non-literate as distinct from illiterate, and in this may lie many of their strengths: their directness and simplicity, their vitality and passion. Ballads were composed in and for a small community, sometimes the court, but more often a working-class, rural community, one having a shared history and shared fears, shared emotions and aspirations, and a shared language or dialect. This being so there would have been some falling-off in their composition as social conditions changed and more and more families left the villages where they had been born in order to work in towns and cities, where broadsides, often scurrilous in content, were winning the day. Many ballads must have been lost forever due to this, but the tradition never completely died out as we can see from the works of Clare and Hardy. Gradually the eighteenth century began to see a renewal of interest in them, even of serious critical interest, and surprisingly the first person to do so was a man whom we now look back upon as being the very embodiment of neo-classicism: Joseph Addison.

It was in May 1711, the same year which saw the publication of young Alexander Pope's *Essay on Criticism*, that Mr Spectator's Paper No 70 urged his readers to look again at 'the old song of Chevy Chase', telling them that, 'I know nothing which more shews the essential and inherent Perfection of Simplicity of Thought, above that which I call the Gothic Manner in Writing.' By 'Gothic' he meant the affectation of unnecessary complexity, that 'false wit' of the likes of Cowley, and which Johnson was later to castigate so famously, and those writers whom Pope also condemned, writers who:

> to conceit alone their taste confine,
> And glittering thoughts struck out in ev'ry line:
> Pleased with a Work where nothing's just or fit;
> One glaring chaos and wild heap of wit.
>
> (*Essay on Criticism* 289-292)

The views expressed by Addison are not so much the earliest hint of that chimera, pre-Romanticism, as an essential part of the literary debate which was establishing neo-classical ideals. His readers might have been surprised to find him making serious textual comparisons between 'Chevy Chase' and Virgil, but it is slightly less surprising when we recognise it as part of the debate between Ancient and Modern. The point he is seeking to establish is that any work of art which has pleased so many disparate generations over a long period of time must have great intrinsic merit, a point which he makes very clearly in Paper 74: 'The sentiments in that Ballad are extremely Natural and Poetical, and full of the Majestic Simplicity which we admire in the greatest of the Ancient Poets.'

Curiously, while it is evident that Addison's influence in the ballad revival is considerable, it is also evident that his views were intended to give full-blooded support to orthodox neo-classicism. But it was not a line of thought which met with universal approval. Johnson, in his *Life of Addison,* observed, in his most forthright manner, that in putting forward such ideas he had 'exposed himself to ridicule', adding that 'In *Chevy Chase* there is not much of either bombast or affectation; but there is chill and lifeless imbecility. The story cannot possibly be told in a manner that shall make less

---

[21]Samuel Johnson, *The Lives of the English Poets,* II, p147-148

impression on the mind.'[21]

During the previous century ballads had been insinuating themselves into various miscellanies, anthologies, garlands and drolleries, along with historical chronicles, bawdy narratives, love lyrics and drinking songs, but in the early years of the eighteenth century they established their independence in the three volume *A Collection of Old Ballads* (1723-25) in which ancient precedence was claimed on the grounds of Homer himself having been a blind old ballad-singer; but without doubt the most influential collection was that edited by Thomas Percy, *Reliques of Ancient Poetry, 1765.*

The Rev Thomas Percy (1729-1811) was appointed to the living of Easton Maudit, Northamptonshire, in 1753, a position he held for 25 years. He was an industrious young man with strong literary ambitions. He published a Chinese novel which he had translated from the Portuguese; he produced a new translation of the Song of Solomon and edited the poems of the Earl of Surrey; but what established his reputation was the discovery he made in 1753: a seventeenth-century folio manuscript commonplaces book of popular songs and ballads. A memorandum, which he wrote on the cover and dated 7 November 1769, tells how he found it: 'This very curious Old Manuscript in its present mutilated state, but unbound and sadly torn etc. I rescued from destruction, and begged at the hands of my worthy friend Humphrey Pitt Esq, then living at Shifnal in Shropshire ... I saw it lying dirty on the floor under a Bureau in the Parlour, being used by the Maids to light the fire.'[22]

How much was lost to us due to this incendiarist we will never know and Percy himself confesses that being 'very young', at the time he had 'not then learned to reverence it'. But by 1757, in a postscript to a letter to Shenstone he is seen to be taking it seriously:

---

[22]Albert B. Friedman, *The Ballad Revival* (Chicago, 1964), p187

'I am possessed of a very curious old MS Collection of ancient Ballads, many of which I believe were never printed ... Mr Johnson has seen my MS and has a desire to have it printed.'[23]

Johnson had been staying with Percy at Easton Maudit for several weeks and had offered him plenty of advice and promises of help. He had said he would help to select the best pieces, suggested that blank pages should be left between them so that he could then write explanatory notes. He also promised a glossary of obsolete words and phrases. It was a prospect which must have excited Percy, but, sadly, as we learn from a note added later to his letter to Shenstone, 'This promise he never executed, nor except a few slight hints delivered *viva voce* did he furnish any contributions.'[24] This is not totally surprising as Johnson was badly behind with his edition of Shakespeare and in truth he had a fairly low opinion of the ballad form. In his *Dictionary* he is bluntly dismissive 'now it is applied to nothing but trifling verse'. Perhaps he was simply being kind to the young man who, he could see, was fired up with enthusiasm. It is as well that Percy did not know how Johnson was later to parody the simplicity of one of the ballads he had written:

I put my hat upon my head,
   And walk'd into the Strand,
And there I met another man
   Whose hat was in his hand.

However, Percy's was an enthusiasm which Shenstone shared. In a letter to him dated 4 January 1758, he declared, 'You pique my Curiosity extremely by the mention of that ancient Manuscript, as there is nothing gives me greater Pleasure than the Simplicity of style and sentiment that is observable in old English Ballads. If

---

[23]Cleanth Brooks, *The Percy Letters* (Yale 1977), p3-4
[24]ibid, p9-10

aught could add to that Pleasure, it would be an opportunity of
perusing them in your company at the Leasowes, and pray do not
think *of publishing* them, until you have given me that
opportunity.'[25]

Percy was very quick to reply and the two men were soon
exchanging poems, much to the delight of Percy who looked up to
Shenstone as a paragon of good taste. From time to time Percy
would include some of the ballads he had found and Shenstone re-
touched them before sending them back. Little progress was made
until 1760 when Dodsley happened to be staying at The Leasowes
and he and Shenstone were working together on the *Fables.* They
were discussing the latest literary sensation: the publication by James
Macpherson of *Fragments of Ancient Poetry,* which he claimed
were translations of the work of the Gaelic poet Ossian. The
'translation' was in fact all his own work, but just like Chatterton's
later *Rowley Poems,* they had caught the imagination and were to
be an international success. It was during these discussions that
Percy arrived bringing his manuscript of ancient poems with him.
Dodsley instantly saw its publishing potential, but over the following
months Shenstone's letters show that it was he who had taken over
the direction of operations. Just how very practical Shenstone could
be in determining the details of printing and publication comes as
something of a surprise; in a lengthy letter to Percy at the beginning
of October he is quite specific, giving out what amounted to
instructions rather than suggestions. What was to be included and
what was to be left out was, in Shenstone's view, to be his decision.
He proposed grading each piece with one of three marks, insisting,
'I would not have you insert any Poems that sink below the second
mark.'[26] And he could be very blunt: referring to two ballads which

[25]*Letters,* p478
[26]Cleanth Brooks, *The Percy Letters,* p73

Percy favoured, he told him, 'There is evidently not a single particle of poetical Merit in *either*.' He added that, 'this kind of ballad will sink your vessel to the bottom of the sea'.[27] He was equally positive about the layout, the typeface and the engraving of illustrations and text: 'No two long ballads should ever be placed one after the other, lest readers might get bored.' It would be wiser to interpose them with short ones. He was equally adamant on the question of notes, which he felt should be 'totally omitted'.[28] Brief introductions were however considered acceptable, as they provided readers with insights into folklore and customs, changes in the language and in poetic traditions.

Ultimately the final edition contained fewer than half of the ballads and songs in Percy's manuscript. For the rest he and Shenstone scoured the whole country. As Percy put it, 'It is in the remote and obscure parts of the kingdom that I expect to find curiosities of the kind I want.'[29] Many came from Shenstone's correspondents in Scotland. Others came from closer to hand, in Shropshire itself, while Percy even contacted his friend the poet, James Grainger, in the West Indies. Thus, he said, 'we ransack the whole British Empire'.[30] Added to this, Thomas Wharton promised to 'ransack all their hoards in Oxford for me'. And he was also given permission to transcribe ballads from the Pepys Collection in Cambridge.

It was altogether an outstanding achievement and at a time when Pope and Johnson and Theobald were establishing the criteria for critical editions. But in one respect Shenstone was responsible for the objection which was most frequently raised. He had told Percy[31]

[27]ibid, p150
[28]ibid, p74
[29]ibid, p109
[30]ibid, p110
[31]ibid, p72

that he could see no objection to 'improvements', even adding, 'As to alterations of a word or two I do not esteem it a point of *Conscience* to *particularize them* on this occasion.' As a result, as Cleanth Brooks observed, 'to this day Percy's name has remained a byword for bad editing – even dishonest editing'.[32] Professor Friedman even goes so far as to say that his alterations, 'consigned him to the special hell reserved for bad editors'.[33] An unfair charge seeing that most of the blame should be laid on Shenstone. It can, however, be argued that such changes, particularly those of spelling and punctuation, were necessary, as Percy was not aiming at scholars like Brooks and Friedman, but was providing the readers of his own day with an edition which they wanted to read.

Shenstone had told Percy that, 'If I have any talent at Conjecture, All People of Taste, throughout the Kingdom, will rejoice to see a judicious, a correct and elegant Collection of such Pieces – for after all, 'tis such Pieces that contain the true Chemical Spirit or Essence of Poetry.'[34]

And he was not wrong in his conjecture. The time was right for such a collection. There had been a groundswell moving in that direction for many years, one early impetus being the work of William Stukely, the archaeologist whose findings on excavations at Stonehenge, published in the 1740s, excited much interest in Druids. Druids were not then associated with grisly images of human sacrifice; they represented an ancient culture. In 'Lycidas' Milton had called them 'old bards, the famous Druids' (l. 53). In 1757, Thomas Gray added to the interest with his ode 'The Bard' and Richard Bentley provided the abiding image of the bearded poet hurling himself from a clifftop. Gray had become fascinated

---

[32]ibid, p*xvi*
[33]Friedman, p205
[34]*Percy Letters*, p77

by Icelandic and Welsh verse forms, but the Ode, he tells us, was prompted by a visit to Cambridge in 1757 by the blind Welsh harpist John Parry.

Alongside this movement was the feeling that didacticism in poetry had gone too far. In the introduction to his *Odes on Various Subjects* (1746) Wharton had argued that 'The fashion of moralising in verse has been carried too far, and as he looks on Invention and Imagination to be the chief faculties of a Poet, so will he be happy if the following Odes may be look'd upon as an attempt to bring back Poetry into its right Channel.'[35]

And it was not only among what one might term the professional literati that changes were taking place. As Stephen Matthews tells us in an intriguing new study,[36] *Josiah Relph of Sebergham, England's first dialect poet,* there was in Cumberland at that time a country curate by the name of Josiah Relph, who was not only writing poems in his local dialect but translating Horace into it too, and with a directness and immediacy surpassing many a metropolitan academic. The opening lines of Ode IV:7 *Diffugere nives* becoming:

> The snow has left the fells and fled
> Their tops i'green the trees hev' cled,
> The grund wi' sundry flowers is sown,
> And to their stint the becks are fawn.

Another strand was the growing interest, down in the south, in all things Scottish – perhaps rather surprising in view of the 1745 rebellion. Even Johnson had been prepared to leave London and travel to the Western Isles, and we should also notice a little known poem by William Collins, 'An Ode on the Popular Superstitions of

[35]Neil Curry, *Six Eighteenth-Century Poets* (London, 2011), p217
[36]Stephen Matthews, *Josiah Relph of Sebergham* (Carlisle, 2015)

the Highlands of Scotland, Considered as the Subject of Poetry', in which, a decade before the appearance of *Ossian*, he tells a friend that he might find old songs:

> Whether thou bidd'st the well-taught hind repeat
>> The choral dirge that mourns some chieftain brave,
> Or whether, sitting in the shepherd's shiel,
>> Thou hear'st some sounding tale of war's alarms.

The time was, therefore, right for Percy's *Reliques,* but only because they *were* Reliques. Had the same verses been offered as new work, the public reaction would have been very different. The violent emotions portrayed in them were acceptable only because they were in the past. Readers were happy to accept this view of the nation's past as an English tradition which suggested that it was not necessary to turn to the classics to find poetic authority. This was something which Chatterton was quick to recognise when he turned to writing his *Rowley Poems* and there is something of a parallel too in Horace Walpole's initial fear that the reading public would not take to the Gothic gloom of his *Castle of Otranto* unless he fed it to them as being a 'translation' of an ancient Italian manuscript.

In that it opened the way to an appreciation of ballads, Percy's *Reliques* could be said to be one of the most important books of the eighteenth century. Vicesimus Knox in his *Essays: Moral and Literary* was in no doubt as to the significance of the changes: 'Verses, which a few years past, were thought worthy the attention of children only, or of the lowest and rudest orders, are now admired for that artless simplicity which once obtained the name of coarseness and vulgarity.'[37]

Most importantly, what it did eventually lead to was, of course,

---

[37]Vicesimus Knox, *Essays: Moral and Literary* (London, 1782), p.214

the *Lyrical Ballads*. In his 'Essay supplementary to the Preface', Wordsworth freely acknowledged his debt:

> I have already stated how much Germany is indebted to this work; and for our own country, its poetry has been absolutely redeemed by it. I do not think there is an able writer of verse of the present day who would not be proud to acknowledge his obligation to the Reliques. I know that it is so with my friends, and, for myself, I am happy on this occasion to make a public avowal of my own.

Among his friends, of course, was Coleridge, whose *Rime of the Ancient Mariner* is the finest and most famous ballad in the English language.

The volume was published as, and is always referred to as, *Percy's Reliques,* but much of the credit, as we have seen, for the contents, layout and critical comments, must go to Shenstone, as Percy himself acknowledged. In a letter dated 30 August 1763 to his friend, Lord Hailes, he declared that he intended 'to inscribe [to Shenstone's memory] the whole collection, as being undertaken at his request, and the plan of it formed under his eloquent super-intendance'.[38] But eighteen months later, when it was published, the dedication, written by Samuel Johnson, was to the Countess of Northumberland. Percy was eager to confirm his family roots, even though he had been born Thomas Piercy. Nevertheless, in his Preface, he did write, 'The plan of the work was settled in concert with the late elegant Mr Shenstone, who was to have borne a joint share in it had not death unhappily prevented him.'[39]

But this is, to say the least, somewhat ungenerous, allowing only the faintest recognition of the immense amount of work Shenstone had put into the project. It is quite evident from their

---

[38]Brooks, p*ix*
[39]*Percy's Reliques of Ancient English Poetry,* ed. Gilfillan (Edinburgh, 1858), p*xxiv*

correspondence that Percy had very little idea of how to edit such a collection, yet it bears his name only. He took all the credit. Likewise, very few of those who bought and extolled Dodsley's anthology had any way of knowing the extent to which the hand of Shenstone had guided the final three volumes.

The literary world has always been competitive and in the eighteenth century no one competed more strongly than Pope and Johnson, to the extent that each had an 'Age' named after him. Of course Shenstone could never be regarded as one of the major players, but, as I hope I have indicated, his own literary achievements, the invaluable assistance he gave to others, and the regard in which so many regarded him as an arbiter of taste, do not merit his having slipped so far down in the ratings. Of a retiring nature, and having retired to The Leasowes, he never asserted himself. Another contributory factor, and one which his friends laid to his charge so often, was his indolence. It does seem that he was incapable of finishing anything on time. Deadlines were never met and when he died there was yet one more unfinished project on his desk, one which was completely unknown until 1952, when Ian A. Gordon published *Shenstone's Miscellany, 1759-1763.*

For several years Shenstone had been collecting poems from his friends and copying them neatly into a notebook. The idea had first occurred to him in 1750. Writing to Richard Graves with a request for some of Anthony Whistler's poems, he explained:

> My reigning toy at present is a pocket-book, and I glory as much in furnishing it with the verses of my acquaintances, as others would with bank-bills.[40]

There is now no trace of that particular pocket-book. However in 1759 he made a fresh start. Writing this time to Richard Jago,

---

[40] *Letters,* p294

> ... any new copy of verses of your own, or of your friends ... I have
> thought of amusing myself with the publication of a small Miscellany
> from neighbour Baskerville's press .[41]

This small, leather-bound notebook of some 200 pages has
survived. On Shenstone's death it had been sent to Thomas Percy,
who added copious notes and annotations, but made no attempt
to have it published. When he died, it passed through various hands,
was auctioned at Sotheby's in 1884, and ended up the library of
Alexander Turnbull, a collector living in Wellington, New Zealand,
who bequeathed it the University Library there.

Among its pages are, as we would expect, verses by many of his
friends: Jago, Graves, Whistler, Percy, Somervile and Lady
Luxborough. But there are also poems by Richard Lovelace, Fulke
Greville, Thomas Wharton, Horace Walpole, Lady Mary Wortley
Montague, Swift and Pope. They show a wide variety of verse forms:
epigrams, pastorals, songs and ballads. It is not, it has to be said, an
exciting collection, but it is evidence of those qualities which he so
valued: simplicity, elegance and portrayals of the essential innocence
of country life; values which before long would become the hallmark
of a new age, but an age which, sad to say, knew little or nothing
about him.

[41]ibid, p503

# 6

# THE LETTER WRITER

SMALL, SELF-CONTAINED COMMUNITIES HAVE LESS NEED for letters; people can talk to each other. It is when the lines of communication get so spread out, as in the case, for example, of the Roman Empire, that its leaders – in contrast to the rulers of ancient Athens – depend upon letters to keep them informed about what is going on thousands of miles away. But it is an added joy to learn that among the thousands of fragments unearthed at Vindolanda was a letter telling us that one of the soldiers stationed there had been sent a new pair of sandals, some socks and two pairs of underpants, no doubt very welcome in a Cumbrian winter.

But a distinction needs to be made between letters and correspondence. Saint Paul no more expected a reply to his letters to the Corinthians or the Thessalonians than the Roman poet Horace did when he wrote his verse Epistles. A correspondence needs a postal service. The concept of the Royal Mail in this country can be said to have originated in 1516 when Henry VIII established the role of 'Master of the Posts', but it was not until 1635, in the reign of Charles I, that it was made available to the general public, which, in practice of course, meant the aristocracy. It was Charles II who founded the General Post Office in 1660, which widened the scope. Then in the early years of the eighteenth century mail coaches began to operate. Initially they only travelled between Bath and London, but it was not long before they were to be seen in almost every town in the country.

It is the eighteenth century which is now looked back upon as the golden age of letter-writing: the age of Horace Walpole, Lady Mary Wortley Montagu, Gray, and Cowper. In their hands it became a literary genre, but it is Alexander Pope who must be credited with having made it so. Before then, to publish one's letters had seemed somewhat immodest, not to say presumptuous, but Pope, devious self-publicist that he was, saw a way round this. Having anonymously fed the press with the tantalising rumour that a collection of his letters was about to be published, he professed to be outraged by this invasion of his privacy. They might not even be letters he had actually written, he argued. Such a dilemma. What was he to do? The only way to protect his reputation, he insisted, was to publish an authorised edition himself. Of course, with such publicity, it was an instant success. Pope had, in the months before this, been asking friends to return copies of his letters to him and had been busy re-writing and improving them. The way was now open for Walpole, Gray and the others.

A new literary genre had been created. But it did not stop there. A small-time printer by the name of Samuel Richardson, having brought out a book to show the less well-educated how letters should be written, saw a new possibility. The result was his novel *Pamela* (1740). Henry Fielding promptly satirised it with *Shamela*, but the epistolary novel was soon flourishing and has never stopped. Equally unstoppable, it seems, is Gilbert White's *The Natural History of Selborne*, with more than 300 editions since its first appearance in 1789, and it too is made up of letters.

It was in 1769 that William Shenstone's letters were first published by James Dodsley, Robert having died in 1764, the year after Shenstone. Even at that date James Dodsley felt the need to justify the publication of 'Letters, not intended for the Public' against the charge that it was 'a violation of Private Friendship'.[1] But, he argued:

> ... the talents of this Author ... were so uncommon, and the fame of his little Ferme ornée under the conduct of a taste entirely original, was to become so considerable, that every specimen of the one, and every anecdote relative to the improvement of the other, seemed too interesting to be buried in oblivion.

And, furthermore he added, that the recipients of the letters 'esteemed it not only a peculiar felicity in their fortunes, but likewise some degree of credit, to have enjoyed the pleasures of such a Friendship through so considerable a period of human life'.[2]

This was not a view altogether shared by everyone and shortly after the book's appearance, Thomas Gray, in one of his frequent snobbish moods, wrote to his friend the Rev Norton Nicholson:

> I have read an 8vo volume of Shenstone's letters, poor Man! he was always wishing for money, for fame & other distinctions, & his whole philosophy consisted in living against his will in retirement, and in a place which his taste had adorned, but which he only enjoyed when people of note came to see and commend it. His correspondence is about nothing else but this place & his own writings with two or three neighbouring Clergymen, who wrote verses too.[3]

As the volume was very limited and did not, for instance, include

---

[1] William Shenstone, *The Works,* Vol III, p*vi*
[2] ibid, III p*x*
[3] Gray, *Letters,* III, p227

any of Shenstone's letters to Thomas Percy, there is, it could be said, some excuse for what Gray says. Shenstone's nineteenth century editor, George Gilfillan, went even further, however. As we have already seen, he did not appear to be enjoying the task he had undertaken. He rarely had a good word to say for Shenstone, and his condemnation of the letters was caustic. He was prepared to grant that they did give us some pleasant 'glimpses of a life and a society which have been dead for a hundred years', but his overall view is one for which a better term might be spiteful:

> His Letters are filled with the little complaints, the little gratifications, the little journeys, the little studies, and the little criticisms, of one whom indolence and rustication had reduced to a little man … The worst thing in Shenstone's correspondence is a small querulousness … His very misery is of a Lilliputian nature.[4]

But against this, and weighing more heavily in the balance, is Samuel Johnson's assertion that 'Shenstone was a man whose correspondence was an honour'[5] and delivered on a day when he was, according to Boswell, in a 'critical' mood. Johnson had just been told that when Richard Whistler died, all Shenstone's letters to him had been destroyed by his brother. If this was an event which upset Johnson, it was one which 'mortified' Shenstone himself, and in his letter saying as much to Richard Graves we learn how seriously he regarded letter writing and the value he put on his own. Indeed his distress is such as to suggest that he already had in mind the possibility of their publication at some time.

> I confess to you, that I am considerably mortified by Mr John Whistler's conduct in regard to my letters to his brother; and rather than that they should have been so unnecessarily destroyed, would

---

[4]Gilfillan, p*xix*
[5]Samuel Johnson, *Life*, II, p452

have given more money than it is allowable for me to mention with decency. I look upon my letters as some of my chef-d'œuvres, and, could I be supposed to have the least pretensions to propriety of style or sentiment, I should imagine it must appear, principally, in my letters to his brother, and one or two more friends. I considered them as the records of a friendship that will always be dear to me, and as the history of my mind for these twenty years past.[6]

Shenstone was not always so serious and solemn. He recognised the potentially comic side of the epistolary style and while he did not go quite so far as Johnson, who held that anyone who tried to read Richardson for the story would hang himself [7], he did find him 'tedious', cheekily suggesting that it was because he was a printer that his novels were so long.[8] He thought *Pamela* 'would have made one good volume'[9] Like Henry Fielding, he recognised how silly it sounds when Pamela uses the present tense to narrate events which were said to be happening there and then, and in a letter to Richard Jago his own parody falls not far short of the brilliant *Shamela*.

> Well! and so I sat me down in my room, and was reading *Pamela* [and] in comes Mrs Arnold – 'Well, Mrs Arnold,' says I, 'this Mr Jago never comes – what can one do? I'm as dull as a beetle for want of company.' 'Sir,' says she, 'the hen – ' 'What makes you out of breath?' says I, 'Mrs Arnold, what's the matter?' 'Why, Sir,' says she, 'the hen that I set last-sabbath-day-was-three-weeks has just hatched, and has brought all her eggs to good.' 'That's brave indeed,' says I. 'Ay, that it is,' says she, 'so be and't please G – d an how they liven, there'll be a glorious parcel of 'em. Shall I bring 'em up for you to see?' says she. 'No, thank ye, Mrs Arnold,' says I; 'but aren't ye in some apprehensions from the kite, Mrs Arnold?'[10]

[6] *Letters*, p412
[7] Johnson, *Life*, II, p175
[8] *Letters*, p.267
[9] ibid, p82
[10] ibid, p28-29

And so it goes on.

While letters in the eighteenth century came to be recognised as an art form, some written to Shenstone by his friend Lady Luxborough were so beautifully illustrated that they could be considered as works of art in their own right. Audrey Duggan has reproduced one, challengingly written in her perfect French, and where the margins are delicately and minutely decorated with hand-painted flowers and tableaux of elegantly dressed eighteenth-century society figures. Small wonder that Shenstone kept all her letters, even, as Dodsley tells us in the 'Advertisement' to his edition, having had them bound together.

Shenstone was a skilled artist himself and the illustrations in the various editions of 'The School-Mistress' are his own, but he never decorated his letters to that same extent. Where necessary he illustrated them, as when discussing at some length with Lady Luxborough the appropriate dimensions, design and inscription for a garden urn in memory of their friend, the poet William Somervile. It was clearly important to him that his letters looked well, in case, as he admitted to her, that they did not read well. 'I love to have my Scrip of Paper well ornamented without, for fear it should have no Merit within.'[11] Seals were of particular importance to him – he had at least seven different types – and he was 'not entirely satisfied unless the sealing-wax itself be of a lively orange scarlet'. Lady Luxborough once kindly sent him a recipe for yellow wax. The vexed question of pens also gave rise to a lively exchange. Lady Luxborough had written to say that she was having trouble with her quills:

> Permit me to interrupt what I am saying with a curse against crow-pens. If I was to add to the curses in the Service for Ash Wednesday,

[11]ibid, p184

the crows would be loaded with them, or rather, the men who invented putting their quills to this use [12]

Geese and turkeys, she insisted, were much better and went on to flatter Shenstone by suggesting that 'the quill [with which] you wrote to me must have been a phoenix in disguise'.[13] Not to be outdone in the fields of flattery, he continued the theme by proposing that the most appropriate quill for Her Ladyship might be that of a blackbird[14], 'a Bird that has both Spirit and Elegance in his Notes'. Or a wood-lark, or going even further, a nightingale. But whatever quill she used, even that of a bittern, she 'could not write disagreeably'. And he concludes that, 'Against the time I write in verse, I nourish a very fine peacock whose harmonious Voice agrees to a tittle with my Versification.' The raucous screeching of a peacock being of course anything but harmonious.

A good deal of quill and ink was employed in those days by correspondents telling each other how they thought letters should be written. In his essay 'On Writing and Books' Shenstone had urged that 'The style of letters perhaps should not rise higher than the style of refined conversation.' On the other hand, he argued, they should never sink too low, and in an interesting comparison declares 'I hate a style, as I do a garden, that is wholly flat and regular; that slides along like an eel and never rises to what one can call an inequality.'[15]

Time and again we hear him complaining that people are not writing to him often enough. He complains to Richard Graves, 'It is a long, long time, according to the computation of friendship, since I had the pleasure of a line from you; and I write chiefly to

---

[12]Lady Luxborough, *Letters Written to William Shenstone* (London, 1775), p72
[13]*Letters*, p74
[14]ibid, p183
[15]*Works*, II, p178

remind you of it.'[16] It is clear that he needed letters. Not long after he first moved into The Leasowes we find him writing a long letter to Graves about his neighbours[17]: ' … their conversation gives me no more pleasure than the canking of a goose, or the quacking of a duck'. He admits that he could be accused of vanity, but, as he wrote on another occasion, 'The truth is I write to please myself.' And he was prepared to write about himself too, as he told Jago:

> I should be ashamed to reflect how much I have dwelt upon myself in this letter, but that I seriously approve of egotism in letters: and were I not to do so, I should not long have any other subject. I have not a single neighbour that is either fraught with politeness, literature, or intelligence.[18]

He had been living at The Leasowes for over a decade then, but evidently things were no better. He did not want to live in the city, certainly not London, but living in the country, at least before he began serious work on his garden, held few pleasures for him. 'The absence of entertainment is a positive pain to me,' he told Graves. 'The man is curst who writes verses and lives in the country.'[19]

Horace Walpole, arguably the finest of the eighteenth-century letter writers, being the son of the Prime Minister, and living as he did, could write movingly and amusingly of the great events of the day, as well as of court gossip and scandal, but for Shenstone life was altogether different. 'The notable incidents of my life,' he complained to Jago, 'amount to about as much as the tinsel of your little boy's hobby horse.'[20]

---

[16]*Letters*, p345
[17]ibid, p32
[18]ibid, p32
[19]ibid, p27
[20]ibid, p128

But this difference is, it could be argued, where the strength of Shenstone's letters lies. It is a strength he came close to recognising himself when he advocated the value of 'cheap amusements'. He advised Jago:

> I would have you cultivate your garden, plant flowers, have a bird or two in the hall (they will at least amuse the children), write now and then a song, buy now and then a book and write now and then a letter.[21]

It is, to a large extent, his own lifestyle he is recommending and in writing about it he has given us a lasting picture of what it was like to be a country gentleman in the middle years of that century. In many respects, as we discover, life was harder then, especially in winter. We would be regarding it as an emergency situation if, like Lady Luxborough, we found our ink frozen in its pot and our fingers so cold that we could not hold a pen anyway. And then there were times when the roads between The Leasowes and Barrels were impassable on account of snow or mud, and their servants – their usual method of delivery – simply could not get through.

Such weather also prevented friends from visiting, and then the isolation could lead to loneliness and depression. As he put it to Graves once:

> I agree with you entirely in the necessity of a sociable life in order to be happy...solitude has exceedingly savage effects on our dispositions.[22]

And the melancholy he so often complained of did have an effect on his health. Health – his own and that of others – is a frequent topic of his correspondence, but that is perhaps not surprising. A trip to the chemist usually cures us of those minor ailments which,

---

[21]ibid, p129
[22]ibid, p195

were they to persist like Lady Luxborough's headaches, and with no easy remedy available, must have been very debilitating. But the 'disagreeable symptoms'[23] in his nerves which alarmed him do suggest that he was something of a hypochondriac, as he went close to confessing as much to Graves:

> I thank God, I have recovered a tolerable degree of health this spring; though by no means free from so much heaviness and lassitude, as renders me averse to all activity of body and mind. In the course of my disorder, so long as I could bear to think of any sublunary enjoyment, I remembered my friends, and of course thought much of you, but its advances were so precipitate, when I sent for the physicians, that I soon received a wrench from every object of this world … I suppose that you have been informed that my fever was in great measure hypochondriacal; and left my nerves so extremely sensible, that, even on no very interesting subject, I could readily think myself into a vertigo: I had almost said an epilepsy, for surely I was oftentimes near it.[24]

He would have expected to be looked after, but the extent to which he depended, and imposed upon, his servants comes a shock. He did not mind travelling, he explained to Jago, as long as it was only a short distance, but could not face the idea of a night away from home:

> … the nights away from home would be insupportable to me. I have fatigued Mrs Arnold's assiduity, to the injury of her health; by occasioning her to sit in my room a'nights, light my candle, put it out again, make me perspiratory wheys, and slops; and am amused by the most silly animadversions she is capable of making. I never knew her usefulness till now; but I now prefer her to all other of her station.

Those words *usefulness* and *station* stick in one's gullet

---

[23]ibid, p480
[24]ibid, p67

somewhat. Yet the situation was by no means unique. We are reminded of William Cowper's treatment of his 'companion' Mrs Unwin, who was very much his equal in station, yet in a letter to his cousin, Lady Hesketh, he described how Mrs Unwin slept in a corner of his bedroom in her clothes. And this went on for twelve years. He admits that 'it is a long time for a lady to have slept in her clothes and the patient at first sight seems chargeable with much inhumanity who suffers it.'[25] At first sight, he says! Inhumanity? How could anyone behave in such a way?

Lady Luxborough, it is worth noting, took great care of her servants, putting off a visit from Shenstone and Lord Dudley on account of one of them having had a stroke:

> ... my old servant Price is struck with a palsy, and one half of his body is dead, so that he is entirely helpless and as his weight and size do not agree with the narrowness on my garret-stairs, there was not a possibility of carrying him, last Saturday, higher than the first storey, where he has continued ever since in the bed Mr Outing lay in till then ... This accident, and the consequences of it, perplex me a good deal, but it was unavoidable for so faithful old servant could not be sent out of the house, unless inhumanity had guided me, which I hope will never be the case, though I forfeit my own pleasure, for I cannot ask to see you and Lord Dudley, where I could not lodge you.[26]

The old servant lasted a little over two weeks. Death in those days was never far away. Both Shenstone's parents died at an early age and his brother Joseph died in his thirties, so he could be said to have had good cause for concern.

But Shenstone's letters are by no means all gloom. Recalling the summer of 1752, he writes:

[25]Neil Curry, p102
[26]Lady Luxborough, p315

> I drank, purchased amusements; never suffered myself to be a minute without company, no matter what, so it was but continual … an almost constant succession of lively and agreeable instants … It was inebriation all.[27]

And it was not the only time he admitted to being drunk. After a visit to a neighbour, 'a return home through the dark found myself vertiginous before I was aware'.[28]

One visit which, understandably, he looked back upon with great pleasure, took place in 1746 and was from 'that right friendly bard', as he called him, James Thomson, who praised his place 'extravagantly' and invited him to his house in Richmond.[29] Thomson died shortly after so the visit never took place, but it was an event Shenstone never forgot and which he commemorated with an inscription on a seat on his Virgil's Grove.

In view of his collaboration with Dodsley on the anthologies, it is surprising and disappointing that there are so few references in his letters to other poets of his day. *The Dunciad* is dismissed as 'flat in the whole' and the product of 'Mr Pope's dotage' and he seems to have shared the general disregard for Gray's later pieces, recommending to Thomas Percy 'if you love mischief, the two odes that ridicule Gray and Mason's manner'.[30] Of his own poems he is dismissive, telling Lady Luxborough that they 'in general smell too much of King-cups and Daffodils'.

But it is in his letters to his friends that we encounter the most fascinating pieces: the gossip, the chit-chat and the anecdotes. We learn of one of the local parsons so ferocious both in temper and zeal that in the middle of a sermon 'he rounded on a Most noble

---

[28]ibid, p355
[29]ibid, p106
[30]ibid, p299

and renowned captain', accusing him of snorting and sneezing, calling him 'a beast and a hog'. On another occasion he told the tiny children belonging to another parson that they were damned for being seen out of doors on a Sunday, and he frequently referred to Halesowen as Hell's-Own.

In contrast, Shenstone seems to have been unable to raise his voice or get cross with anybody. One of his tenants had gone three and a half years without paying any rent and he supposed he ought to do something about it, but doubted if he would 'both through indolence and compassion'. His compassion may have been stretched somewhat by another tenant who agreed that 'he would pay me half a year's rent (at a time when he owes me for two years) but that he could not fix any time because he was unwilling to break his promise'.[31] Perhaps he saw the funny side of this high moral stance.

His compassionate nature was never more obvious than in a long letter he wrote to his friend the actor and playwright Thomas Hull in 1761. He reminds him of an incident that had taken place the previous autumn when his fish-pond had been robbed. He had declined to prosecute the offender and was now being accused by several of his upright landowning neighbours of screening a robber from justice and giving encouragement to future thefts. 'Such are the aspersions with which I have been loaded,' he tells him. There ought, he argues, to be a real distinction made between as robber and a pilferer. And in words which remind us of Christ's parable, he adds, 'Nor can I assign the former Appellation to a poor Wretch, who, in his Hunger, has taken two or three Fishes or as many Loaves.' He admits that at first he was so angry that he could have punished the man himself, but

---

[31] ibid, p137

... when the Warmth submitted to cool Reflection, I felt it impossible to resist his Argument of having a Wife with five Children at Home, and not a Doit to procure them a Meal. I verily believe too he spoke the Truth. Poverty and Affliction seemed to work and plead within him, and his Words were the Words of Nature ... The poor Fellow subsists, chief Part of the Year, only by carrying News-papers round the country. Had he been shut up, what was to have supported the ragged family?[32]

Having started on this train of thought, he went on to show himself decades ahead of his time on the subject of capital punishment:

I have suffered myself sometimes to doubt the Excellence of our Laws, relative to Life and Death, notwithstanding I know it has been asserted by many People, that they are wiser than those of any other Nation. What then? Is the Man who takes a few Guineas from you on the Highway, on a level with him who commits a deliberate Murder? And is there no punishment to be found more adequate to the first Transgression, than taking away the Life? Surely, one Example made by a visible Brand, a mark of Disgrace, which could never be washed away, would more avail towards the Prevention of future Crimes, than half the Executions in the Kingdom, which have now, from too great Frequency, lost the chief Part of their Purpose and Terror.[33]

One might look upon Shenstone as being a little naïve in his belief that a brand would be sufficient to shame criminals into mending their ways, but just how far ahead of his time such enlightened thinking was becomes evident when we consider that by the end of the century there were almost 200 capital offences on the statute books, and they included the theft of goods valued at twelve pence and even 'crimes' as strange as being in the company

---

[32]ibid, p605
[33]ibid, p65

of gypsies for one month.

Another story telling of his benevolence appeared in the *Birmingham Mirror* in 1823 and related that a man with a pistol had accosted him in his own grounds and demanded money. The lady who was with him fainted away, but Shenstone handed over his purse saying that money was not worth struggling for. However, he sent one of his servants to follow the man and he reported back that on reaching home the poor fellow had flung down the purse, telling his wife, 'Take it, I have ruined my soul to keep you from starving.' On finding that he had previously been hard-working and of good character, Shenstone not only forgave him, but employed him as a labourer on the estate. Even if untrue, and it was written many years after his death, it does show the light in which people remembered him.

When it came to practical, business affairs, such as editing, selection of texts, printing and publishing, his letters to Dodsley and Percy, as we have already seen, could be counted on for clear thinking, positive decisions and efficiency, even if coupled at times with a degree of lethargy. He could always be relied upon to complete a task, even if, like one of his tenants, not necessarily on time. But even his most practical letters are rarely without some piece of chit-chat and it is these seemingly minor events which give us new insight into the times. For instance, we learn that in July 1743, 'A malignant caterpillar has demolished the beauty of all our large oaks. Mine are secured by their littleness but the park (Hagley) suffers; a large wood near me being a mere winter-piece for nakedness.'[34]

And without letters of this kind we might never have known, as Lady Luxborough informs us, that 'the late King George (George

---

[34]ibid, p27

I) was fond of peaches stewed in brandy in a particular manner, which he had tasted at my father's, and ever after, till he died, my mamma furnished him with a sufficient quantity to last the year round (he eating two every night)'.[35]

But what we learn of one of the foibles of eighteenth-century polite society is such as to leave us scratching our heads in bewilderment. Shenstone tells Lady Luxborough:

> I had a letter from him (Richard Graves) yesterday, dated at London, wherein he tells me that the most extraordinary Instance of Modern Politeness is the Pantin – a sort of Scaramouch made with Card, which the ladies bring into Company and the Playhouse – he makes their Compliments for them and serves them for Amusement – the Duke of Newcastle brought one into the Privy Council, as the Report goes.[36]

One's first reaction is that Graves must have been joking, but Lady Luxborough's reply confirms that people were actually carrying around life-sized puppets. Her reaction is to scoff at the notion:

> I am in doubt, when I hear of this polite fashion, whether it is a mark that the world is returned to its infancy (as old people grow childish) or whether it be not some coquettish invention, that Mr Pantin may say in dumb show what the Lady who wears him cannot say for herself.[37]

But such is the power of fashion that in her very next letter we learn that she is about to have one of her own. What's worse, she is clearly excited at the prospect.

> At last I am in the fashion, and have got a Pantin. Miss Patty Meredith

---

[35]*Letters*, p140
[36]Lady Luxborough, p26
[37]ibid, p32

writes me word that she sends me a Pantin of the newest sort, and
that the woman who sold it assured her it was just arrived in England,
and is reckoned to make as genteel curtsey as any Monsieur in
Europe.

And if Pantins were not enough to convince us that their world
had indeed returned to its infancy, she goes on to tell of another
fashion:

> There is another of later date that is worthy of admiration; for there
> is a party of gentlemen and ladies of fashion who entertain the
> company at Vauxhall with the most charming harmony. The ladies
> crow like cocks, and if any gentleman of the party are within hearing,
> they answer them by braying like an ass.[38]

And these are times which have variously been called 'The Age
of Elegance' and 'The Age of Reason'. Shenstone avoided the topic
in his next letter to her.

Shenstone's friendship with Lady Luxborough was one of the
chief events and a turning point in his life. It was Richard Jago who
introduced them in 1739. Shenstone was then 25 and she was 39,
but it was a friendship which grew over the years, bringing a
contentment and, one might say, a joy into what might otherwise
have been rather solitary lives. His first reaction on being introduced
to her was a touch of pride, not to say vanity, and when she paid a
visit to The Leasowes he told Jago that 'A Coach with a coronet is a
pretty kind of phenomena at my door ... few things prettier.'[39]
And in his early letters to her the self-deprecation and deference
border on the obsequious, but as the years pass the tone relaxes
and while he always addresses her as 'Your Ladyship', there is
occasionally a little flirtatious touch on both sides. It is, however,

[38]ibid, p109
[39]ibid, p273

part of a game. Flirtatious letters had been the cause of her downfall and she would never risk further embarrassment and social obloquy.

They had so many interests in common, as they were to discover. Their gardens, as one might expect, took up a good deal of their correspondence, but that is better left to a later chapter.

It was evidently important to both of them that things should be done properly so that when their friend, the poet William Somervile, died and Lady Luxborough decided to erect an urn to his memory in her garden, letter after letter passed between them debating the issue to ensure that the dimensions, the design and the inscription were exact and proper in every way.

Similarly the furnishing and decoration of their rooms was a matter of concern, especially the cost:

> The Case is, I have been amused (shall I say, or fatigued rather) for these six weeks with a Considerable Crowd of Workmen. I believe I told your Ladyship in my last, that having completed my schemes for the year out of Doors, I was then beginning upon my House. I have not been a Day since that time without two Masons & their Attendants, two Carpenters & sometimes three, a Painter, Plummer, glazier & the Lord knows who beside. My House is a bottom-less Pit, as Swift said formerly of the Law: Or rather it is a whirlpool which sucks in all my money & and that so deep that there in not the least glimpse of it appears through the water.[40]

Lady Luxborough was pleased to announce that she had found a way of saving money when decorating her ceiling. She explained the process:

> I am assured that the paper carvings are quite as beautiful, and more durable, than either wood or stucco, and for ceilings infinitely preferable, especially as they may be moved, being only fastened up with tacks. They adorn chimneys and indeed whole rooms with them,

---

[40]ibid, p273

and make picture-frames of them. The paper is boiled to mash and pounded a vast while, then it is put into moulds of any form, – but further I know not, only that when it is tacked up, you either paint it white or gold, as you would do wood.[41]

And as she goes on we realise that papier-maché has just been invented.

Poetry was also important to them both and from the earliest days of their friendship, Shenstone had been sending copies of his poems to her, which for the most part delighted her, but she was never slow to voice a disagreement. The Preface he proposed for his Elegies was something she took against.

I confess, the length of the Preface gave me some pain, lest the impatience of many readers might make them lay down the book before they got to what that is meant to introduce them to and in some persons it may raise scruples as to the propriety of Elegies, which they would not ever thought of objecting to.[42]

It is a valid objection. Her advice could at times be very practical indeed. She suggested, and with reason, cutting the final four stanzas of Elegy XIV, but Shenstone thought otherwise. She also questioned the ending of Gray's 'Elegy', a view many have shared: 'I cannot tell who wrote the Verses in a Country Churchyard, but I like them well and think the first part of the Elegy very beautiful. I cannot see why it did not end at the most beautiful line in it.'[43] Unfortunately she does not say which line she thinks that to be.

And on another occasion she tells of something which might be of interest to Handel scholars: 'Handel has told me that the hints of his very best songs have had once suggested several of them been owing to the sounds in his ears of cries in the street.'[44]

---

[41]Lady Luxborough, *Letters*, p80
[42]ibid, p58
[43]ibid, p292
[44]*Letters*, p150

But it is perhaps the day-to day occurrences recorded in their letters which give them such charm. As was often the case Shenstone had sent a servant to Barrels with one of his letters and was expecting her return, but her Ladyship had not finished her reply in time and apologises for keeping her overnight, adding, ' I have sent her to see my Gardens and Coppice, but fear she will despise them, being used to yours.'[45]

Lady Luxborough had once suggested using pigeons to carry letters between their houses but Shenstone rejected the idea:

> I am pleased with your Ladyship's Project concerning Pigeons, but we must not practice it. Old Emma would inevitably fire her Musquet at them, tho' I believe at the same time that she hardly knows a Gun from a Besom.[46]

Emma was Emma Scudamore, who Shenstone explained was:

> An old-woman who goes from my Neighbourhood three Times a Week to Birmingham, with a single Exception all the year round. Her business is, to bring hither from the Post Office every thing that is directed to this Part of the Country. And, as she calls me her Best master, and knows how gladly I receive a Letter &c she seizes what is directed to me with eagerness and rapidity.[47]

Lady Luxborough refers to her as 'the ambulatory old gentlewoman' and those words suggests that she walked from The Leasowes to Birmingham, which being at least 12 miles there and back, was rather more than an amble.

Even Emma seems to have had a sense of how important her mission was and a letter Lady Luxborough wrote in the severe winter of 1753 puts it beyond doubt:

[45]Lady Luxborough, p130
[46]Lady Luxborough, p360
[47]*Letters*

Though I undertake to write to you to-night, I do not know how
my letter is to be wafted to Birmingham, unless some kind Sylph
offers her service, the terrestrial messengers not being able to travel,
at least not in this country, where it snows, rains and freezes, not
alternately, but at the same time. Is that your case in Shropshire? If
so, I pity you, but I think you and I who have not much else to do,
should utter our lamentations to each other from the corners of the
same chimney. Sharing the burthen of winter would lessen it to
each of us.[48]

Less than eighteen months later, and having written more than
120 letters to her friend, Lady Luxborough died. Other than a formal
acknowledgement of the news we have no record of how he reacted
to it, but his grief at such a loss can be imagined. At least he had
kept all her letters and could read them over again, for as he had
once written, and with some feeling evidently, among his aphorisms:

In a heavy oppressive atmosphere, when the spirits sink too low,
the best cordial is to read over all the letters of one's friends.[49]

[48]Lady Luxborough
[49]*Works*, II, p262

7

# THE LANDSCAPE GARDENER

IN HIS MODESTLY-TITLED ESSAY *UNCONNECTED Thoughts on Gardening* (published in1764, but written several years before that) Shenstone wrote, 'Gardening may be divided into three species – kitchen-gardening – parterre-gardening – and landskip, or picturesque-gardening'[1], and the OED has credited this as being the earliest recorded use of the term 'landscape-gardening'. It is a term we are so familiar and comfortable with now that we may fail to see how startling it must once have been. A landscape is something 'out there' in the distance, something we look at, but which we are not part of. It pre-exists us. In contrast, a garden is something small which we can be 'in' and which encloses us. It is also a construct, something we can shape to our own design. Putting the two together involves not only a change in perspective, but in thinking. How did this come about?

There is, seemingly, something about gardens which prompts people to want to write about them, hence garden historians have

---

[1] *Works*, Vol II, p125

had little difficulty – even when the actual gardens themselves may no longer exist – in tracing how these changes came about. Clearly we have no evidence as to the origin of the very earliest gardens, but we can assume that it would not have taken long for the first settled communities to see the advantage of having vegetables and herbs close to their homes rather than have to go looking for them. But a garden which is non-productive and exists solely for pleasure? Such a garden could come into existence only when and where there is a degree of peace and prosperity, where there is enough land which the owner can afford to set aside for pleasure, a luxury which would be out of the question were that land in danger of invasion. Peace and prosperity, but it must also be a time when a high value is placed on culture as well as cultivation.

We talk of land being 'tamed' without always seeing the implications of that metaphor. To tame is to domesticate and domestication invariably involves domination, thus to a greater or lesser extent all gardens are about subjecting nature to our own whims and wishes. And at times some of these whims have had a touch of eccentricity to them. The Romans had a passion for topiary – forcing trees into shapes which nature never intended them to have. It was a passion they brought with them to England and which persisted as we can see from the garden at Levens in Cumbria, that astonishing collection of Alice-in-Wonderland sculptures in yew.

Wealth played its part, as is evident from the medieval walled gardens which feature so strongly in love poems such as 'Le Roman de la Rose' and in parodies of them too: Chaucer's 'Merchant's Tale' being a famous example. They gave privacy to a privileged few – a rare luxury one imagines in the crowded life of a castle.

All gardens are artificial, and few more so than the complex geometrical designs of Tudor knot-gardens. They cry out, 'Look at me!' They are about showing off; they are demonstrations of social standing and power.

It is this ostentatious display of power which is behind the great Renaissance gardens of Italy and never more so than in the Villa d'Este at Tivoli. It was constructed in the 1550s by Cardinal Ippolito d'Este who, having failed to be elected pope, seems to have been determined to demonstrate to his rival that he could live on a far greater scale and could out-spend him at every step. The steep hillside overlooking the Albueno Valley was cleared of all vegetation – and people – to establish the grandiose terraces which support the fountains: over 500 separate jets, ranging from the elegant avenue of 100 fountains to that magnificent piece of hydraulic engineering, the Organ Fountain, where water directs compressed air through organ pipes sequenced so as to play four different tunes. Water and stone. What the garden does not have is flowers. Nature has been excluded, save for a few wild cyclamen growing under the clipped box hedges. As Horace Walpole put it in his essay 'On Modern Gardening', such gardens were '… unnatural, enriched by art … and were anything but verdant and rural'.[2]

If medieval gardens – especially those in monasteries – were meant for quiet meditation, the Villa d'Este was meant to awe. Vaster and grander of course is Louis XIV's Versailles which became a setting for display, pageantry and performance and was planned not so much to awe as to over-awe, which it exhaustingly still does. The English, and quite rightly, regarded

----

[2]Horace Walpole, *On Modern Gardening* (Pallas Guides), p15

Louis XIV as a megalomaniac and a tyrant – traits fully apparent in his 'garden' – and their reaction against what they also saw as a Roman Catholic extravaganza was therefore not only a matter of fashion but of politics. The gardens of England, home of Liberty, were to become 'natural'.

Walpole, never one to be shy of giving voice to his opinions, was scornful of these foreign fads:

> Art, in the hands of rude man, had at first been made a succedaneum to nature; in the hands of ostentatious wealth, it became the means of opposing nature; and the more it traversed the march of the latter, the more nobility thought its power was demonstrated. Canals measured by the line were introduced in lieu of meandering streams ... Balustrades defended precipitate and dangerous elevations ... Vases and sculpture were added to those unnecessary balconies and statues furnished the lifeless spot with mimic representations of the excluded sons of man.[3]

And by quoting at length William Temple's fulsome praise of the extravagancies of the Countess of Bedford's garden at Moor Park he brought equal scorn down on English imitations of them. But Moor Park was not, seemingly, the worst example of its kind.

> We have seen what Moor Park was, when pronounced a standard. But as no succeeding generation in an opulent and luxurious country contents itself with with the perfection established by its ancestors, more perfect perfection was still sought; and improvements had gone on till ... absurdity could go no further, and the tide turned.[4]

Charles Bridgeman (1690-1738), who completely re-designed

---

[3] ibid, p22
[4] ibid, p40

Lord Cobham's estate at Stowe, is credited by Walpole with initiating this movement towards gardens which blended seamlessly with the surrounding countryside – with *Landscape Gardens* as they came to be called. Walls and boundaries were done away with, we are told, by that 'capital stroke', the invention of the *ha-ha*. In truth, Walpole was wrong on this point as it was a Frenchman, Guillaume Beaumont, who had dug the first such ditch at Levens Hall in Cumbria in 1695. But Bridgeman's use of it was far more adventurous and effective; it set gardens free that they might 'assort with the wilder country without'.[5]

But Walpole's greatest praise is reserved for the remarkable William Kent. Born in 1686 in Bridlington in Yorkshire, his career began as a painter of coaches and inn-signs, until some local gentry, spotting a different talent, sent him to be trained in Rome, where he is known to have painted a church ceiling and theatrical scenery. There he met Richard Boyle, Earl of Burlington, who was on his Grand Tour; Kent became his guide and an unlikely life-long friendship – with no trace of homosexuality – developed between them. They returned to England with a love of Italian landscape and of the Italian landscape painters Claude and Poussin, a love which they first brought to bear on the design of the Earl's garden at Chiswick.

Burlington was regarded as the paragon of good taste. It was to him that Alexander Pope addressed his Fourth Moral Essay *Of the Use of Riches*, an essay which contains those two famous statements on gardening: 'In all, let Nature never be forgot' and 'Consult the Genius of the Place in all.' The *beau monde* was quick to follow Burlington's example, as we can see from a letter

---

[5] ibid, p43

by Sir Thomas Robinson, the owner of Rokeby Hall in Yorkshire. A keen gardener-designer himself, he told his father-in-law, the Earl of Carlisle at Castle Howard, that a garden by Kent, 'when finished, it has the appearance of beautiful nature, and without being told one would imagine art had no part in the finishing'.[6] Walpole's assertion has become famous:

> ... born with a genius to strike out a great system from the twilight of imperfect essays. He leaped the fence and saw that all nature was a garden.[7]

Walpole was, of course, writing this essay in 1770, after the completion of these events. As he says, 'It is not my business to lay down rules for gardeners, but to give the history of them.'[8] But the name which is missing, totally and surprisingly, from Walpole's history is that of the man who had the imagination to advocate such changes and to foresee their social and economic possibilities: Joseph Addison, an unlikely pioneer, having been a city-dweller, a civil servant and a journalist.

It was in a set of ideas published in *The Spectator* during the summer of 1712 that he put forward some challenging ideas. His starting point was that 'There is something more bold and masterly in the rough, careless Strokes of Nature, than in the nice Touches and Embellishments of Art.'[9] but qualified it by accepting that ' ... tho' there are several of these wild Scenes, that are more delightful than any artificial Shows, yet we find the works of Nature still more pleasant, the more they resemble those of Art'. Among the embellishments he is opposed to is

---

[6]Tim Richardson, *The Arcadian Friends* (London, 2007), p291
[7]Walpole, p43
[8]ibid, p32
[9]*The Genius of the Place* ed, Hunt and Willis (London, 1988) p141

topiary: 'Our British Gardeners … instead of humouring Nature, love to deviate from it as much as possible. Our trees rise in Cones, Globes and Pyramids. We see the marks of the Scissors upon every Plant and Bush.'[10] It was an early suggestion of a new way of looking at things, but to challenge an orthodoxy by positing its virtual opposite demands no great leap of imagination, but such a leap there was from what, in its wording, looked to be no more than a passing notion. He put a question to his readers: 'Why may not a whole estate be thrown into a kind of garden … that may turn as much to the Profit as to the Pleasure of the Owner?'

Without using the term, he had, with these words, given rise to the term *ferme orné* – the ornamental or ornamented farm. To some extent almost every eighteenth-century manor house was a farm. Distances and the state of the roads meant that there was no popping down to the shops. Families had to be as self-sufficient as they could: growing their own fruit and vegetables, possibly harvesting their own wheat and tending to their own livestock, so Addison's suggestion was something of a novelty and certainly a challenge. The term itself suggests that the concept had its origin in France and it could of course be argued that it dates back to the Horatian ideal of *utile dulci*; nevertheless the first Englishman to take up the challenge is said to have been Philip Southcote, who converted almost a quarter of his 135 acre farm at Woburn, near Weybridge, in Surrey to 'pleasure grounds'.

Thomas Whatey, in his authoritative *Observations on Modern Gardening* (1770) tells us that the 'decorations are communicated to every part; for they are dispersed along the sides of a walk,

---

which, with its appendages, forms a broad belt around the grazing grounds, and is continued, though on a more contracted scale, through the arable. This walk is properly garden; all within it is farm.'[11] The 'decorations' included a serpentine river, a bridge, a ruined chapel, a menagerie, seats and alcoves, and a carefully grouped and tiered planting to allow a variety of prospects; the most novel feature being the 'walk' which directed visitors to undertake a specific pictorial circuit. It was this which, indirectly, was behind Shenstone's design at The Leasowes, though The Leasowes was more pastoral and far less ornamental.

It was, admittedly, a very indirect line of descent, dating from 1743 when Shenstone visited the home of his university friend Richard Graves at Mickleton in Gloucestershire and was impressed by the changes which had been made to the gardens, changes which had been suggested by a relative who had visited Southcote's farm. A tenuous link, but sufficient for Graves to assert in his *Recollections* that 'this was, however, sufficient to engage the attention and the active imagination of Mr Shenstone'.[12] Sufficient for him to write to Graves some five years later that 'The French have what they call a *Parque ornée* ... I give my place the title of a *ferme ornée*, though, if I had the money, I should hardly confine myself to such decorations as the name implies.'[13]

Shenstone had been only ten when his father died and he inherited The Leasowes, an inheritance which cannot have meant much to him at that time. The Rev Thomas Dolman, a relative

---

[11] Thomas Whately, *Observations on Modern Gardening* (London, 1770) p177-178

[12] Graves, p50

[13] *Letters*, p156

on his mother's side, became his legal guardian and took over the management of the estate, while William, who was never again to enjoy any family life, went off to boarding school in Solihull and then in 1732, the same year in which his mother died, to Oxford. On coming of age in 1735 he left university without taking a degree and returned home, but not to The Leasowes, which had been leased to a distant relative, John Shenstone. He shared the house for a while but eventually moved into Harborough Hall, a timbered Elizabethan manor house which had been the home of his mother's family for more than two centuries. In the years that followed he seemed unable to settle, confessing in a letter written in 1736 to his cousin Maria Dolman, 'I am at present in a very refined state of indolence and inactivity. Indeed I make little more use of a country life than to live over again the pleasures of Oxford and your company.'[14] He had an inheritance of £300 a year and, as Graves put it, he thought it 'better to enjoy ease and independence with a competent fortune, than to toil, and be subject to the caprice of others'.[15]

It was, as we have seen, his visit to Mickleton which had aroused his interest in gardening, but there was no comparison between Mickleton and The Leasowes in 1743 when he wrote to Graves:

> If a poet should address himself to God Almighty with the most earnest thanks for His goodness in allotting him with an estate that was over-run with shrubs, thickets and coppices, variegated with barren rocks and precipices, or floated three parts in four with lakes and marshes, rather than such an equal and fertile

---

[14] E. Monro Purkis, *William Shenstone* (Wolverhampton, 1931), p24
[15] Graves, p35

spot as the 'sons of men' delight in; to my apprehension he would be guilty of no absurdity.[16]

It was a promising prospect, however, and when he did move into The Leasowes in 1745 one of the first things he did, Graves tells us, was to cut a straight walk through his woods and at the end of it to construct 'a small building of rough stone, stick a little wooden cross on it and call it a hermitage'.[17] It was a beginning, and while the straight walk suggests a rather formal approach, the hermitage shows the part which imagination and decoration were to play in all his subsequent plans. Compared with estates such as Chatsworth and Stowe, The Leasowes was miniscule, but over the next eighteen years he transformed it into one of the most famous and influential gardens in the country. As Graves put it, 'Few men have risen with so rapid a progress, and on apparently so slender a foundation from a state of the utmost obscurity to so great a degree of celebrity and repute as Mr Shenstone.'[18] And what he says is so true. The Leasowes became a garden which had to be visited by the expert as well as by the curious.

In 1755 he told his friend Robert Binnel that ' ... though I first embellished my Farm, with an eye to the Satisfaction I should receive from its Beauty, I am now grown dependent on the Friends it brings me'.[19] And when winter came and travel became difficult he was lonely without them; it has also to be said that they appealed to his vanity, as he confessed to Jago, 'It is now Sunday evening and I have been exhibiting myself in my walks

---

[16]*Letters*, p70
[17]Graves, p.51
[18]Graves, p7
[19]*Letters*, p451

to no less than a hundred and fifty people, and with no less state
and vanity than a Turk in his seraglio.'[20] And his letters to Lady
Luxborough are often dominated by accounts of which persons
of quality have been to see him.

One early visit of which he was justly proud was paid by 'that
sweet bard', as he called him, James Thomson. It was in the
summer of 1746 when they were introduced by Sir William
Lyttleton and during their walk through the garden Thomson
was full of praise, yet praise which, so we are told, ended up with
one double *entendre* after another. 'You have nothing to do,'
observed Thomson, 'but to dress nature – you have only to caress
her; kiss her, and then descend into the valley.' This was enough
to set them off. The two hills – Clent and Walton – he suggested
were 'two boobies of nature'. Lyttleton was sure he could see a
nipple on one, and the 'fringe of Upmore Wood' prompted a
joke about the 'gushing stream' which ran near Shenstone's
door.[21]

A very different note is struck by Samuel Johnson who could
see no point in any landscape garden and was at his most sarcastic
in his *Life of Shenstone*:

> Whether to plant a walk in undulating curves, and to place a
> bench at every turn where there is an object to catch the view; to
> make water run where it will be heard, and to stagnate where it
> will be seen … demands any great powers of mind, I will not
> enquire: perhaps a sullen and surly speculator may think such
> performances rather the sport than the business of human
> reason.[22]

---

[20]ibid, p204
[21]McKillop, *Thomson's Visit to Shenstone*, Philological Quarterly 23 July, 1944
[22]Johnson, *Lives*, III, p350

But what else could one expect from such a confirmed townie? And it was raining when he visited The Leasowes with Mrs Thrale, but she herself wrote in her Journal that 'if one had to choose among all the places one has seen, the Leasowes should be the choice to inhabit oneself'.[23] Death had saved Shenstone from having to read Johnson's sullen and surly comments, but he would have been delighted to know that a decade after his demise his gardens would be visited by two future presidents of the United States, Adams and Jefferson, and that John Wesley thought that 'there was nothing in all England to compare with it'.

As has already been shown, it was with the publication of the posthumous two-volume *Collected Works* that Robert Dodsley brought Shenstone to the attention of a wider public, both as poet and essayist. However, in addition, he can be credited with furthering the fame of The Leasowes by including at the close of the second volume an account of the garden together with a fold-out map which established the direction of the circuit Shenstone had wanted visitors to follow and, in doing so, indicated the chief stopping places and points of interest. All subsequent writers on the garden have followed Dodsley's example and to differ and to try to create a time-line of the changes and improvements Shenstone introduced would only lead to a confused picture, as it seems that initially he had no clear aims and objectives. Graves tells us that at first: 'Mr Shenstone had no conception of a whole, or of disposing his environs on any consistent plan'.[24] The garden, one might say, seems to have evolved, to have dictated its own direction.

---

[23]Purkis, p81
[24]Graves, p57

\* \* \*

At Mucklow Hill, on the road from Birmingham to Bewdley, and just outside what was then the village of Halesowen, a narrow lane veered off to the left and, where it turned a corner at the bottom, visitors to The Leasowes found themselves faced by a Gothic Arch known as the Priory Gate, built with stones from the ruins of Hales Abbey. It was a portal to a world so very different from that of Mucklow Hill: a world, if not of fantasy, certainly a world of the imagination and of literature, for Shenstone had provided his visitors with some sixteen seats (often with Classical quotations attached) where he hoped they would sit, contemplate the scene before them and quietly meditate upon it.

In the foreground of Shenstone's own watercolour of the Gate there is a pilgrim or possibly a hermit complete with rosary and crucifix, suggesting a somewhat romantic retreat to earlier and gentler medieval times. In his own times he had the practical problem of unscrupulous visitors picking his flowers and so on a nearby roothouse, he appended a poem in which 'rural fays and fairies' threatened anyone who dared offend in such a way; the last stanza reading:

> And tread with awe these favour'd bowers
> Nor wound the shrubs, nor bruise the flowers;
> So may your path with sweets abound!
> So may your couch with rest be crown'd!
> But harm betide the wayward swain,
> Who dares our hallow'd haunts profane.

In his *Unconnected Thoughts on Gardening*, Shenstone had

written that 'In gardening it is no small point to enforce either grandeur or beauty by surprise,'[25] and after we have followed a little cascade down through the tree-lined Priory Walk it is certainly a surprise to come out on the edge of the Priory Pool. For one thing, *Pool* is a misnomer; this is a substantial lake, large enough to be home to families of coot and mallard. The surprise element also fulfils another of his *Unconnected Thoughts*: 'Water should ever appear as an irregular lake or a winding stream', and what he has designed meets both criteria. It would seem that the Pool was one of Shenstone's last projects. As late as 1760 he is telling Graves of 'the workmen (of whom I have fourteen or fifteen this very day) making a piece of water below my Priory'[26] and complaining to Thomas Percy that the project had 'confin'd me, employ'd my servants, and enslav'd my horses all this Year – I hope to finish it the next week'. But he was being optimistic. The following year he is still saying, 'the grand water will make no figure till next spring'.[27] Sadly, it seems he may never have seen it as he wished, as after his death it was still 'not compleated', according to Dodsley.

A Priory Walk to a Priory pool presupposes a priory, and a priory there was, but one constructed by Shenstone himself in 1757 on some higher ground above the pool. Several years previously, the Lyttletons, his wealthy neighbours at Hagley, had commissioned Sanderson Miller to build a truly splendid full-scale Gothic castle for them. Shenstone had been somewhat critical of it at first. 'There is no great Art or variety in the Ruin,

[25] *Works*, II, p144
[26] *Letters*, p556
[27] ibid, p588

but the Situation gives it a charming Effect,' he had written to Lady Luxborough,[28] adding a pencil sketch to prove his point that the Chief Tower was ten feet too low! But later he had some of his own trees chopped down so that he could have a view of it.

Ruins were an important feature of many an eighteenth-century garden and in his *Uncollected Thoughts* he had written, 'A ruin for instance may ... afford that pleasing melancholy which proceeds from a reflexion on decayed magnificence ... Ruinated structures appear to derive their power of pleasing from ... the latitude they afford the imagination.'[29] His own ruin was comparatively modest, but had a utility factor in that it incorporated a small cottage which he rented to an elderly couple for £4 a year. There were, however, some authentic touches: the stone again came from Hales Abbey, but he also incorporated some of its window frames. The inside, as can be judged from an inventory made later by his friend John Scott Hylton, must have been surprisingly like an actual chapel. As well as the Gothic shields mounted around the cornice and which Shenstone describes in a letter to Lady Luxborough, there was a Gothic chimney piece above which he had hung a bass relief crucifixion fashioned in alabaster. Stained glass had been added to the window frames. There was a carved figure of Christ crowned with thorns and over the door a carving of a martyred bishop. In addition there was a painted wooden triptych depicting the adoration of the Magi in the centre and flanked by images of saints.[30]

Finally, he also provided his visitors with 'Gothic chairs', an

---

[28]ibid, p148
[29]*Works*, II, p131
[30]*Letters*, p497

indication of how he wanted them to approach his garden: not to hurry on from one feature to the next, but to sit and contemplate, to meditate on its air of quiet nostalgia, its religious melancholy. Sadly, we cannot do this, as all that now remains of that priory are some rather impressionistic watercolours and black and white photographs. In 1965, some brain-dead functionaries, deeming it to be unsafe, rather than taking steps to secure it, had it totally demolished instead. Ah, those tasteless, senseless sixties. As Ruskin had written more than a century before, 'It may hereafter be a subject of sorrow, or a cause of injury, to millions that we have consulted our present convenience by casting down such buildings as we chuse to dispense with. That sorrow, that loss we have no right to inflict.' Yet 30 years later, he added a despairing footnote 'any more wasted words than mine throughout life, or bread cast upon more bitter waters, I never heard of'.[31]

But we can still, if we wish, enjoy the rural scene outside and sit quietly for a while on the nearby Meliboeus' Seat, which takes its name from a quotation from Virgil's *Eclogue VII* (one of many throughout the garden) which is to be found inscribed on it and which, in translation, reads:

> Come hither, Meliboeus, your goat and kids are safe and if you can find time for idling, take your rest beneath the shade.

And if we do take his advice and idle away some time there, we will notice an urn. Urns were another significant feature of gardens at that time. This one, dedicated to his friend, the poet William Somervile, is a very portly affair – solemn, large and

---

[31] Ruskin, *Selected Writings* (Oxford 2004), p79

plain – as he had told Lady Luxborough such urns should be. They exchanged letter after letter about the urn she had been planning to commemorate Somervile in her garden at The Barrels.[32]

Next are the cascades, and thanks to an account in Graves's *Recollections* we have a clear picture of just what an effort went into the creation of The Leasowes as visitors came to know it:

> This cascade was absolutely no more than a mere ditch, or hedgerow of hazels and other common brush-wood, but, by clearing away the briars and thorns, and shewing the water busily huddling down amidst the roots, and glittering through the stems of the trees, it has an uncommonly beautiful effect.[33]

The Great Cascade, he goes on to tell us, 'falls near twenty feet, among some broken rocks or fragments of stone' and delighted Dodsley who called it, 'a fairy vision'. In a letter to Graves he says of it, 'its appearance well resembles the playfulness of infancy; skipping from side to side, with a thousand antique motions that answer no other purpose than the amusement of their proprietor'.[34] The Earl of Stamford was present at the opening of this cascade and spoke so highly of it that Shenstone had a root-house built there and dedicated it to him.

The path then leads us to what Shenstone used to call his 'forest ground' and while Joseph Heely's description of it is rather lush it shows just how it struck contemporaries:

> The interweaving of the branches of the trees, and the disposition of them form a kind of long Gothic arch, with pendant foliage, as

---

[32]Duggan, p71
[33]Graves, p60
[34]*Letters*, p628

you have seen ivy from the breaks of an old ruin ... and the water rushing from the farthermost part of it, within the deepest gloom, is truly romantic ... Its character is a mixture of the savage and the sprightly, worked up into such perfection that it is out of the power of genius and taste to go farther.[35]

It was here that Shenstone positioned a statue of Faunus, the horned Roman deity of the wildwoods. It had been a gift from Dodsley. A statue of Pan was also to be close by, but both were vandalised – vandalised, it is suggested, by someone outraged by such a blatant display of paganism. It is a suggestion given comic credence in Graves' novel *The Spiritual Quixote*, in which an itinerant Methodist preacher by the apposite name of Wildgoose, visits The Leasowes and not only knocks down Mr Shenstone's statues, but opens his sluices and destroys his cascades.

Dodsley it was who designed the inscription on an urn commemorating Shenstone's younger brother, Joseph, who had died of pneumonia in 1751. They had been very close and Shenstone was deeply affected by his death. Again a quotation from Virgil's *Eclogues* was chosen: 'Now that the Fates have taken you away, Apollo has left our fields, and Pales too.'

From here the path begins to rise, giving views over the opening countryside, but according to Dodsley Shenstone feared that there might be 'some want of life in this part' and so erected another Gothic Seat with a twelve-stanza poem attached, stanzas two and three reading:

> Learn to relish calm delight,
> Verdant vales and fountains bright;

---

[35]Joseph Heeley, *Letters on the Beauties,* p119

Trees that nod on sloping hills,
Caves that echo tinkling rills.

If thou can'st no charm disclose
In the simplest bud that blows,
Go, forsake thy plain and fold,
Join the crowd, and toil for gold.

The path continues to rise towards a group of fir trees which overarch an octagonal seat, giving eight very different views of the landscape and on the back of which there is a goblet inscribed 'To all friends round the Wrekin', an old Shropshire toast which refers to a custom whereby a large group of people held hands to form a human chain round the Hill, which can be glimpsed about thirty miles away.

Beyond this the Gothic theme returns with a Hermitage – few eighteenth-century gardens were complete without one. Writing to Lady Luxborough in July 1749 he was able to tell her that, 'My Gothic building is now completed … the Floor of it is pav'd Carpet-Fashion with black and white Pebbles; & considering how hastily I collected & dispos'd them, has a pretty good Effect.'[36]

To all intents, Shenstone could be seen, as was posited in Chapter One, to be living the Horatian Ideal and at the top of the hill were the most famous of all expressions of it: the opening lines of Horace's *Satire II.6*:

This was what I had prayed for: a small piece of land
With a garden, a fresh-flowing spring of water at hand
Near the house, and, above and behind a small forest stand,
But the gods have done much better for me, and more –
It's perfect. I ask nothing else.

---

[36]*Letters*, p207

From there one ought to be able to look down onto the house where he lived out this ideal. There is a house, but it is not his house. His was demolished by a Mr Edward Horne in 1776, who then built the house we see today, which is in fact the Clubhouse of the Halesowen Golf Club, and, ironically, has become a listed building because of its 'Shenstone connections'. (There is nothing to suggest that Shenstone ever played golf!)

In contrast comes the long shady, tree-lined pathway known as *Lovers' Walk*, where, as Joseph Heely put it, 'one would wish to linger and to live'.[37] Here we find the *Assignation Seat* with another quotation from *Eclogue VII*. Heely, letting his emotions get the better of him, tells us it was 'suitably adapted for the cooing of those fond turtles who might occasionally meet there', and speculated that Shenstone himself had perhaps spent 'his leisure hours here with a favourite nymph in amorous dalliance'. We would like to think so – Mary Cutler, perhaps.

However, this path was also the site of one of the saddest features of The Leasowes, the beautiful memorial urn dedicated to his cousin, Maria Dolman, his 'best beloved and most accomplished of relations'. When only 21 she had died from that most awful of deaths, smallpox. The urn describes her as his 'most lovable kinswoman' and 'the most elegant of maidens'. And on the back of it are those sombre words *Et in Arcadia ego*.

At the top of the hill visitors would have been grateful for another seat and would have doubtless agreed with its Virgil quotation *Divini Gloria Ruris* (The glory of the divine countryside). From there, and after pausing to look into a Temple of Pan, Arcadia was indeed waiting for them: Virgil's Grove.

---

[37]Heeley, p169

In terms of basic facts, Virgil's Grove is simply a thickly-wooded, steep-sided dell with a small stream running down through it, a stream which at its widest point twists and runs round two tiny islands – they are really no more than rocks – and is then crossed by a diminutive single-arch bridge. But these facts do nothing to account for the atmosphere of the Grove, a feeling of something almost approaching sanctity, and such that one instinctively speaks in a whisper. Nothing could appear more natural, yet it is, in fact, Shenstone's masterpiece (he even added the two rocks himself) which every step and every Virgilian quotation have been leading to.

The stream enters the Grove by way of the truly impressive Great Cascade, roaring out of a grotto green with fern and liverwort before tumbling more than twenty feet into a deep pool shaded with trees.

At the entrance to the Grove stands an obelisk declaring '*p.virgilio maroni/lapis iste cum luco sacer esto*' ('To Publius Virgilius Maro let this stone and grove be dedicated'). Also commemorated in yet another quotation from *The Eclogues* is James Thomson and his visit to The Leasowes in 1748. A seat in his honour has an inscription beginning, '*Quae tibi, quae tali reddam pro carmine dona?*' ('What gift can I give you in exchange for such a song?')

Thomas Smith painted a view of the Grove, but it is drab and lifeless, whereas Shenstone's own watercolours, albeit rather gawkishly amateurish, have a warmth to them which manages to capture something of its romance and which support Dodsley's assertion that 'I believe none ever beheld this grove, without a thorough sense of satisfaction; and were one to chuse any one particular spot of this perfectly Arcadian farm, it should, perhaps, be this.'[38]

A gravel path then took visitors up to the house where refreshments would have been waiting once they admired the shrubbery – a word which, it is thought, Shenstone may again have been the first to use.[39] We have perhaps a mistaken idea of shrubberies. They were not all composed of evergreen shrubs. A tedious poem, *The Leasowes*, written by Shenstone's protégé James Woodhouse catalogues peonies, roses, daffodils, narcissi, even raspberries and exotics such as the tulip tree. Dodsley gives us a more vivid picture:

> Thus winding through flowering shrubs, beside a menagerie of doves, we are conducted to the stables. But let it not be forgot, that on the entrance to this shrubbery, the first object which strikes us is a Venus de Medicis, beside a bason of goldfish, encompassed round with shrubs.[40]

Shenstone's visitors took away with them not only vivid memories, but also ideas they could incorporate into their own estates. As Michael Symes observes, he inherited ' ... a run-of-the-mill farm, nothing more and developed it into a landscape garden which won world renown'.[41] His influence was considerable. In the eight years of his close friendship with Lady Luxborough they exchanged some 200 letters and they were mostly about their gardens, she seeking advice about The Barrells and he giving it. As she once declared, 'You are the only touchstone of true taste that I can have recourse to here.'[42] But

---

[38]Heely, p169
[39]*Works*, II, p365
[40]*Works*, II, p336
[41]*Works*, II, p369
[42]Lady Luxborough, p186

we also learn from one of his letters to her in 1749 that 'The Earl of Stamford call'd on me with three Gentlemen this week to see my walks … He was much struck with Virgil's Grove, and particularly the Cascades.'[43] And it was its cascades for which the Earl's garden at Enville was later to become famous. On Shenstone's death the Earl renamed one of its most impressive ornamental buildings 'Shenstone's Chapel' and Sir George Lyttleton erected an urn in his memory at Hagley, facts which give the lie to Timothy Mowl's ill-informed and dismissive assertion that, 'It would be an error to take Shenstone's achievement at The Leasowes too seriously.'[44]

William Shenstone died at the age of 48 – possibly from influenza – on Friday, 11 February 1763 and sadly the demise of The Leasowes began from that very moment. As there was no immediate family the estate went to a distant relative, John Hodgetts, who cut down much of the timber, sold it off and then promptly sold the whole estate. Oliver Goldsmith was only slightly exaggerating when he wrote that it went through ten owners in as many years, including a slave ship captain and a Birmingham button-maker. By 1773 it was, he said, in a 'ruinous situation'. But even he did not foresee that three years later a Mr Edward Horne would pull down Shenstone's house and build a new one. Things were not helped when a sixty foot embankment was built allowing an extension to the Birmingham and Worcester canal to cut across the bottom of Priory Pool. Desecration had not finished however: Major Francis Halliday – yet another owner – decided he could improve on Shenstone's

[43] *Letters*, p255
[44] Timothy Mowl, *Gentlemen Gardeners* (London, 2000) p131

hermitage by extending it and decorating it with cowheel bones and horses' teeth. Further owners appeared on the scene – one going bankrupt – until Matthew Attwood bought the house in 1807 but let the grounds fall into a state of total neglect which lasted for over a century. For a decade it was a College of Physical Education and, in 1906, the Halesowen Golf Club took over what had once been farmland, 'Shenstone's House' becoming the Clubhouse. In 1934 the site was bought by Halesowen Council and it became a public park. Then something almost miraculous happened; it was decided to restore The Leasowes to what it had once been. A Lottery Heritage Grant was applied for and £1,300,000 was forthcoming, to be followed by £1,750,000 from Dudley Council. Professional contractors were brought in and heavy machinery used to restore the paths, the pool, the seats, the stonework and the Great Cascade. It was work done with such care and sensitivity that walking through it today you would not believe that it was other than the garden which Shenstone himself had created and as it has been awarded the status of Grade I on the English Heritage list of parks and historic gardens, its future is, one hopes, now secure.

# 8

## *IL PENSEROSO?*

THE PRECEDING CHAPTERS HAVE SHOWN US Shenstone as a poet, an essayist, an aphorist, an editor, a letter-writer and a landscape gardener, six very different and distinctive roles and yet, had he confined himself to only one of them, he could, I think, be said to have achieved more than most men of his time. Admittedly, it was only as a landscape gardener that he was truly outstanding, but one would not wish to be without any of his multiplicity of talents.

But what do we know of the man who could wear so many hats? We do not *need* to know anything else at all of course, but human curiosity being what it is, we *want* to. And there are writers who, the more we read them, the closer we feel we come to them until it begins to seem like a friendship and, as Stefan Zweig said of his reading of Montaigne, 'The printed page fades from view; a living person steps into the room instead.'[1]

We know what Shenstone looked like, or at least we think we

---

[1]Sarah Bakewell, *How to Live* (London), p7

do. In an early head and shoulders portrait by Thomas Ross we see a slim, elegantly dressed young man looking very self-assured, even a little supercilious. A few decades later, in the full-length portrayal by the Birmingham artist Edward Alcock, he is still elegantly dressed, but he has mellowed considerably: the suave sophisticate is now a country gentleman. We find him leaning casually against a pillar, one hand on his hip, ankles crossed and with his faithful hound Lucy gazing up at him. Seemingly casual, but this is how he *wanted* to be seen. We know this because he sent some sketches to Richard Graves asking him, ' … tell me what you think of some of the attitudes that I enclose'.[2] He also confesses that Alcock had been given instructions to 'lessen my dimensions'. Even so, the portrait is that of a heavily-built man, certainly well-fleshed and in a somewhat lethargic pose. The eyes no longer have the assertiveness of Ross's picture; indeed there is something of a sleepy look about him, suggestive of the indolence he was so often accused of and which he himself readily admitted to.

So which portrait do we hold in our minds, and then what of the thousands of unrecorded images which must have flickered past as the one segued into the other? Virginia Woolf, than whom there was no more precise delineator of character, was acutely aware of the difficulties of biography. 'It is easier to believe,' she wrote, 'that the true life of your subject shows itself in action which is evident rather than in that inner life of thought and emotion which meanders darkly and obscurely through the hidden channels of the soul.'[3] And as Shenstone himself told

[2]*Letters,* p535
[3]Virginia Woolf, *Selected Essays* (Oxford, 2008), p95

Jago, 'The notable incidents of my life amount to about as much
as the tinsel of your little boy's hobby-horse.'[4]

There is one interesting constant between the two portraits in
that, unlike those of his friends Graves, Somervile, Lyttleton and
Dodsley, he is not wearing a wig. One could interpret this as an
indication that he did not much care what people thought of
him, but he seems to have been somewhat self-conscious (Graves
calls him 'bashful'), especially over what he saw as his ungainly
appearance. In a letter to Graves he related that:

> I have been walking in the Mall to-night. The Duke was there,
> and was highly delighted with two dogs; and stared at me more
> enormously than ever Duke did before. I do not know for what
> reason; unless for the same which made him admire the *other*
> puppy-dogs, because they were large ones.[5]

Not wearing a wig might also, I would like to think, suggest
that even in dress he was shaking off Augustan formality in favour
of what was natural and simple, but the only safe conclusion is
that, like the rest of mankind, he was full of complexities and
contradictions, which of course makes for far more interest.

Not wearing a wig must have been more remarkable at that
time than one might expect, as that 'he wore his own hair' is one
of the first things we are told when Mr Wildgoose encounters
Mr Shenstone in Richard Graves' novel *The Spiritual Quixote*
(1773), and features again and at length in his *Recollections*
(1788):

> According to the unnatural taste which then prevailed, every
> schoolboy, as soon as he was entered at the university, cut off his

4*Letters*, p128
5ibid, p46

hair, whatever it was, and, without any regard to his complexion, put on a wig, black, white, brown, or grizzle, as 'lawless fancy' suggested. This fashion no consideration could at that time have induced Mr Shenstone to comply with. He wore his hair, however, almost in the graceful manner which has since generally prevailed … It often exposed him to the ill-mannered remarks of people who had not half his sense.[6]

It is thanks to Graves that we know the little we do about Shenstone's undergraduate days. Students gathered, as doubtless they always have, in various cliques and societies. At Pembroke, he tells us, one group amused itself by reading Greek and drinking water. Another, 'west-country lads', drank good ale, smoked and sang 'Bacchanalian snatches', while elsewhere, gentlemen commoners, 'bucks of the first head', drank port-wine, toasted their girlfriends in punch and 'kept late hours'. Shenstone, he assures us, was often to be found among both the latter groups, but never the water-drinkers.

He was, evidently, a social animal, but not gregarious. After leaving college he spent some time quite happily in London, visiting the theatres and going into coffee houses and in a letter to Jago he invites him to join him there, promising he will 'hear how the eunuch-folk sing' and see the 'Belindas and Sylvias of gay life!'[7] But six years later he has changed his tune, advising Jago, 'I would have you cultivate your garden; plant flowers, have a bird or two in the hall (they will at least amuse your children), write now and then a song; buy now and then a book; write now and then a letter.'[8]

---

[6]Graves, p24
[7]Letters, p35
[8]ibid, p129

Shenstone needed friends. In an early letter written from The Leasowes he complains to Graves about his neighbours, 'their conversation gives me no more pleasure than the canking of a goose, or the quacking of a duck'. The social life of Halesowen was clearly limited and it irked him: ' ... though a very limited number of friends may be sufficient, an idle person should have a large acquaintance; and I believe I have the least of anyone that ever rambled about as much as I have done. I do not know how it is, but I absolutely despair of ever being introduced into the world.'[9] Yet it is clear that he had no time whatsoever for the formalities of social life. We saw in Chapter 2 how boorishly he behaved on a visit to Anthony Whistler; he thought their card-playing was childish and, as for dancing, he used to say it was only allowable in savages. Graves seems to have said he was being too choosey and accused him of vanity, to which Shenstone partly agreed, but replied, 'It is the vanity to be intimate with men of distinguished sense, not of distinguished fortune.'[10]

In later life, however, it has to be said that he was no longer quite so free from vanity. Writing to Graves in 1762 he says, in one of the last letters he ever wrote ' ... we have paid our devoirs to a good deal of genteel company; of which this season has afforded me at least an equal share with any that went before. I will particularise a few.'[11] The list of the *few* which then follows takes up almost a complete page of Marjorie Williams' edition of his letters and includes a quite remarkable collection of well over fifty lords and ladies, together with accompanied earls

---

[9]ibid, p32
[10]ibid, p32
[11]ibid, p638

and counts, not to mention a marquis, the Duke and Duchess of Richmond and a Gentleman of the Bed-chamber to the King of Denmark.

For actual friends, what he wanted was simply the company of a few intelligent and cultured people he could talk to while walking through his grounds or sitting by his fireside: a perfectly normal wish.

What always has to be remembered though in Shenstone's relationship with these friends is his total loyalty. Polonius would have been proud of him, as those he had and their adoption tried, he did indeed grapple them to his soul with hoops of steel. And it was a love and loyalty which was returned.

Richard Jago he had known since they were small boys together at Solihull School; Richard Graves he met when he went up to Oxford. All three kept in constant touch, visiting and writing letter after letter to each other right up to Shenstone's death in 1763. His friendship with Lady Luxborough was of a much shorter duration but between 1739 and her death in 1755 they exchanged more than 200 letters and were involved in almost every aspect of each other's lives. She seems to have regarded him as the arbiter of true taste in all things and rarely made a decision without his support and approval. Similarly, Robert Dodsley, friend and publisher to the likes of Pope, Johnson and Gray, turned to Shenstone for advice on who to include in his anthology. Percy's *Reliques*, as we have seen, would never have achieved the acclaim it did without the – largely unacknowledged – effort and acumen he put into it, and it appears that the renowned Birmingham printer John Baskerville, whose type face is still in use today, might at times have been too dependent, as in 1762 we hear Shenstone complaining to Percy, 'I have been plagued much of late with Designs for the Ornaments for Baskerville's *Horace*.'[12]

Graves sums up his character very neatly when he writes, 'He was the warmest and most affectionate friend, disinterested, liberal and generous in every sense of the word.'[13] But it was not only to those of his own social class that this warm-heartedness and generosity of spirit was shown. His failure to pressurise his tenants into payment of long-outstanding arrears of rent only exacerbated his own financial troubles and he managed to get himself into trouble with some of his wealthy neighbours by refusing to prosecute impoverished wrong-doers even though it was he who had been the one to suffer.

Remarkably for the time, there was no trace of condescension in his dealings with the 'lower orders'. A case in point, as we have already seen, being that of James Woodhouse, a 24 year-old local shoemaker, who sent Shenstone some poems which so impressed him that he took a personal interest in the young man, giving him a key to his grounds and free access to his library, a generosity which Woodhouse gladly acknowledged when his poems came to be published. Johnson took a very different line when he heard of it. According to Boswell, he:

> spoke with much contempt of the notice taken of Woodhouse, the poetical shoemaker. He said it was all vanity and childishness and that such objects were, to those that patronise them, mere mirrors of their own superiority. They had better furnish the man with good implements for his trade, than raise subscriptions for his poems. He may make an excellent shoemaker, but can never make a good poet.[14]

[12]ibid, p619
[13]Graves, p171
[14]Boswell, *Life of Johnson* (London, 1876), p219

It has to be said that when he met him, Johnson's attitude softened and it was perhaps through his influence that Woodhouse became steward to Edward Montague, the husband of Elizabeth, a leading literary figure. Dodsley then helped him to establish a stationery business in Grosvenor Square and also published his poems. It could almost be said that the success of the 'Cobbler Poet' was briefly greater than that of Shenstone. Indeed in 1765 he was invited to dine at Streatham Place, the town house of Mrs Thrale, where one of his fellow diners, also there for the first time, was Samuel Johnson. A final irony being that the announcement of Shenstone's death in the *Arts Gazette* and the warm obituary which went with it were the work of that same James Woodhouse.

Johnson had very few positive things to say about Shenstone. In his *Life*, he claimed that 'His house was mean and he did not improve it,'[15] adding that it was liable to flooding as there was a hole in the roof. Bishop Percy denied all of this: 'Johnson grossly misrepresented both Shenstone's circumstances and his house, which was small but elegant and displayed a great deal of taste.'[16] Johnson even included an extract from one of Gray's tetchy letters in which he claims that Shenstone's 'whole philosophy consisted in living against his will in retirement'. *Against his will?* Graves, who knew him better than anyone, wrote in his *Recollections*, 'I do not think any consideration would have bribed Shenstone to live away from The Leasowes.'[17] It is hard to know what was in Gray's mind.

Retirement. It was one thing for James Thomson, supported

---

[15]Johnson *Lives*, III, p352
[16]ibid, III, p352 Note 4
[17]Graves, p136

by a patron and living comfortably in Richmond, to celebrate it:

> An elegant sufficiency, content,
> Retirement, rural quiet, friendship, books,
> Ease and alternate labour, useful life,
> Progressive virtue and approving Heaven!
>
> (*Spring.* ll 1161-1164)

Or for an outsider such as James Melmoth, who on learning that Dodsley was staying at The Leasowes, wrote to him in June 1759 to say that:

> ... in your present situation you are in possession of a happiness too great for mortals, enjoying in one of the hottest seasons that was ever known in England, the shade and the coolness of the finest groves, perhaps in the world, rendered still more enchanting by the conversation of one of the best poets as well as one of the worthiest men of the age.[18]

But for Shenstone it was an actuality, a daily actuality, and he was well aware of the hazards of its darker side. Initially, as was only to be expected, it was a lifestyle he had some difficulty in adjusting to, as he explained to Graves in 1742:

> ... however I complain, I must own, I have a good deal reconciled myself to this mixture of gratification and disappointment which must be my lot till the last totally prevails.[19]

In the winter when the days were dark and damp and his friends could not visit him, he did find it depressing, and it is not just a touch of the fashionable poetic melancholy we hear him giving voice to in his letters. There were times when he reached the depths:

---

[18] Dodsley's *Letters*, p418.
[19] *Letters*, p44

Now I am come home from a visit – every little uneasiness is sufficient to introduce my whole train of melancholy considerations, and to make me utterly dissatisfied with the life I now lead, and the life which I foresee I shall lead. I am angry and envious, and dejected and frantic and disregard all present things just as becomes a madman to do ... My soul is no more suited to the figure I make, than a cable rope to a cambric needle.[20]

This in a letter to Jago dated 1741, but in his very next letter to him comes the suggestion that they go off to London to see the 'Belindas and Sylvias of gay life'. And against this depression there is an account of his life to Christopher Wren (a grandson of the architect) in 1752:

I neither read nor write aught besides a few letters; and I give myself up entirely to scenes of dissipation; lounge at My Lord Dudley's for near a week together; make dinners; accept of invitations; sit up till 3 o'clock in the morning with young sprightly married women over white port and *vin de paysan;* ramble over my fields; issue out orders to my hay-makers; foretell rain and fair weather; enjoy the fragrance of hay, the cocks and the windrows.[21]

There sounds to be not much wrong with that life; all we can safely assume is that like the rest of us he had his good days and his bad ones. But what is certain is that he knew the hazards of the Horatian Ideal and that it wasn't for everyone. Towards the end of his life he wrote to Thomas Hull, whose uncle had gone to live in an 'obscure part of Essex'. He didn't think it was a wise idea.

He should have remained in the World ... It is most certain that

[20]ibid, p34
[21]ibid, p346

Amusement and employment in themselves, Fancy, Reflection, and a Love of Reading, are indispensably necessary for such a situation. It is downright Lunacy for a Man who has passed his life in a Compting-House, or a Shop … to think of *retiring*. He knows not the Fatigue he is going to encounter: he will want Employment for his Hours; most probably shorten his Existence, and while he retains it, it will be one state of Apathy, if not Disorder.[22]

Idealists be warned

Shenstone was, for the most part, content. He loved reading and kept up to date with what was being published at the time, especially by Dodsley. His garden was clearly a passion and he painted very bold watercolours, both of the garden itself and of its flowers. And he played the harpsichord, once telling Graves that 'music is my dernier resort'.[23] But there was one aspect of his retired life to which he was never fully reconciled and that was the neglect he felt he suffered as a writer as a result of it. And he didn't hold back, telling Graves, 'I am vain enough to imagine that the little merit I have deserves somewhat more regard than I have met with from the world.'[24] And to Jago, 'I cannot bear to see the advantages alienated which I think I could deserve and relish so much more than those that have them.'[25] He knew what the problem was: as a landscape-gardener he had to be in The Leasowes, whereas a writer needed to be in London frequenting the coffee-houses. Only then would he be *known*. It was a state of affairs he had recognised very early on. There was no one in Halesowen he could talk to about his work, no one to

[22]ibid, p608
[23]ibid, p33
[24]ibid, p151
[25]ibid, p34

argue with, to compete with, to spark against. 'The man is curst who writes verses and lives in the country,' he wrote.[26] And there was no easy solution: as a Jewish poet once observed to me, 'With only one arse, you can't dance at two weddings.'

There is little doubt that he could have achieved more if he had asserted himself more. Several times in the letters we hear of his plans to publish a collection of his poems, but he never got round to it. Even Graves saw his initial decision to live at The Leasowes rather than take a degree and follow a profession as tending to be the avoidance of something. As he put it:

> In short, Indolence persuades him … that it was better to enjoy ease and independence with a competent fortune, than to toil, and be subject to the caprice of others, to augment it.[27]

It is somewhat curious that despite having established a renowned garden, written enough poems to fill a substantial volume, as well as letters and essays, and assisted Percy and Dodsley in their editorial tasks, Shenstone is so often charged with indolence. He even accepted the charge when Jago accused him of it: 'You speak of my dwelling in a Castle of Indolence, and I verily believe I do.'[28] He seems to have driven Dodsley to distraction. 'God grant me patience!' he exclaims in one of his letters. Shenstone was seemingly making countless changes to the texts of his own poems and Dodsley remonstrated, 'Why should you alone insist upon that absolute perfection to which no human production did ever yet arrive?'[29]

---

[26]ibid, p28
[27]Graves, p35
[28]*Letters*, p165
[29]Dodsley's *Letters*, p323

More importantly, in the Preface to his 1764 edition of the poems, Dodsley accuses him, and with some justification, of a lack of ambition: 'He chose rather to amuse himself at the foot of the mount, than to take the trouble of climbing the more arduous slopes of Parnassus.'[30]

It would seem that Shenstone had largely himself to blame for a lack of recognition, yet his feeling that he was held in some disregard in certain quarters has an element of truth to it. The Rev George Gilfillan, who does not seem to have warmed to the task of editing Shenstone, wrote in his Preface, 'The Letters are filled with the little complaints, the little gratifications, the little journeys, the little studies, and the little criticisms of one whom indolence and rustication had reduced to a little man.'[31] Physically, we know, Shenstone was anything but little, so where does this scorn (it is far stronger than *disregard*) come from? Gilfillan was writing in 1854, almost a century after Shenstone's death, so must have inherited it from somewhere. Initially the finger wavers in the direction of Johnson, who wrote in his *Life*, 'For a while the inhabitants of Hagley affected to tell their acquaintance of the *little fellow* (my italics) that was trying to make himself admired.'[32] But the chief culprits, I suggest, were Gray and Walpole.

Gray was both patronising and scathing about Shenstone in his letters:

> Poor man! he was always wishing for money, for fame and other distinctions ... and in a place which his taste had adorned, but which he only enjoyed when people of note came to see and

[30]*Works*, II, pv
[31]Gilfillan, p*xix*
[32]Johnson, III, p351

commend it: his correspondence is about nothing else but his
place and his own writings with two or three neighbouring
clergymen who wrote verses.[33]

One can hear the sneer. He had once praised *The School-
Mistress,* but for the rest:

> ...why does he do no better? he goes hopping along his own
> gravel walks, and never deviates from the beaten path for fear of
> being lost.[34]

Consider the implications of that word *hopping.*
Walpole too had read Shenstone's *Letters* and pities him:

> I felt great pity on reading these letters for the narrow
> circumstances of the author, and the passion for fame he was
> tormented with, and yet he had much more fame than his talents
> entitled him to. Poor man, he wanted to have all the world talk
> of him for the pretty place he has made, and which he seems to
> have made only that it might be talked of.[35]

Shenstone was in no need of the great man's pity and the
contemptuous word *pretty* is not one which could ever seriously
be applied to The Leasowes. Walpole certainly did not intend to
give Shenstone any more fame either as there is no mention
whatsoever in his influential book *On Modern Gardening.* And
writing to the antiquary William Cole about Shenstone and his
friends the tone is even nastier, referring to them as:

> puny conceited witlings who give themselves airs from being in
> possession of the soil of Parnassus for the time being.[36]

[33]ibid, p354
[34]Gray's *Letters*, II, p25
[35]Walpole's *Letters*, p150
[36]Humphreys, p358

And why all this nastiness? We do not, I think, have to look far. What else might we expect from two such Old Etonians discussing some grammar school boy (*Solihull? Where in God's name is Solihull?*) who was getting above himself? After all, who were his friends? Some minor clerics who wrote verses. Dodsley, yes, but he had begun life as a footman, hadn't he? And as for Lady Luxborough, Walpole had read her letters:

> She had no spirit, no wit, knew no events; she idolises poor (again) Shenstone who was scarce above her, and flatters him to be flattered.[37]

He might almost have added 'and she was no better than she should be'.

Motivated by snobbery they were wrong in their assessment of Shenstone, just as Johnson was wrong when he asserted, 'I am afraid he died of misery.'[38] *Misery* is a word picked up by Gilfillan, I would suggest, when he observed that 'Even his misery was Lilliputian.' No, he did not die of misery, but if he had, what a wonderful shape it would have given to his life story: the only one of the eighteenth-century Horatian Idealists who had actually *lived* the idea and it hadn't made him happy. It made him miserable. It is potentially such a splendid story that some have seized on Richard Graves's novel *Columella* to so twist it.

In Audrey Duggan's biography we read, 'In his novel *Columella*, Graves models his plot upon Shenstone and the Leasowes household', confidently adding, 'it is understood that the material in all his novels is meticulously replicated from life.'[39]

---

[37]*Letters*, 204
[38]Boswell, p146
[39]Duggan, p35

A.R Humphreys is equally sure that Columella 'undoubtedly represents Shenstone and was recognised as a portrait during Graves's lifetime.' And E. Monro Purkis likewise says, 'Shenstone is admittedly the original of his Columella.'[40]

*Columella* is a terrible novel, a tedious rag-bag of a thing in which Graves was seeking to follow the example of Laurence Sterne. That this is so seems certain from his strong denial of any such thing in his Preface, which, as in Sterne, comes at the end: 'No, Sir, I should despise myself for adopting Sterne's oddities, as much as I do him for affecting the ribaldry and blackguardisms of Rabelais.'[41]

Lucius Columella, who died in AD 40 was, as Graves would have expected his classically-educated readers to know, the most important writer on agriculture in the Roman Empire, his *Res rustica* running to twelve volumes. In Graves's novel it is the nickname given to the protagonist Cornelius Milward by his two visitors on account of his living in rural retirement. *Retirement*, it is worth noting, was defined by Johnson as 'A private way of life, as opposed to an active participation in a trade, a business, a profession, or politics.' There is a slight sense of disapproval in it.

But this Columella is not William Shenstone. It is true that at the outset Graves claims that this is an account of an actual person: 'As the principal subject of the following narrative is a real fact, he begs that it may not be called a *Novel*, or a *Romance*,' novels being that 'species of composition' to which he knows his (probably fictitious) dedicatees are 'professed enemies'.[42]

---

[40]Purkis, p105
[41]*Columella*, II, p242
[42]ibid, I p*v*

But to accept this assertion on its face value as a statement of fact is to make a serious mistake. The conventions of fiction as we know them today, especially that of the omniscient narrator, had not then been established. The early exponents of fiction – Swift, Defoe, and Richardson – all set out by denying their authorship and insisting that they were NOT making things up. The same is true of *Columella*. Graves presents himself not as the author, but as 'the Editor'. It is all rather clumsy but he was very far from being an accomplished novelist. Fiction was not something he understood: his command of dialogue and depiction of character are totally incompetent. What he did understand – he had been doing it most of his life – was how to write a sermon. We will come back to this.

The persona Columella is not William Shenstone but that they share certain aspects of his life – such as his 'aversion to cards'[43] – are not surprising, indeed are perhaps inevitable, as Graves was not good at making things up.

As familiarity with *Columella* is highly unlikely, the rough outline of the 'plot' in Clarence Tracey's *Portrait of Richard Graves* would seem advisable:

> In spite of having been given a good education and of possessing genuine talents, Columella has buried himself in the country, where he toys with landscape gardening and tries to convince himself that he is living an ideal life. Actually he is bored, frustrated and lonely, bothered by his servants and harassed by his neighbours, incapable of the inner serenity necessary for the contemplative life. Eventually, being lonely, he falls victim to the amorous advances of his housekeeper, whom he marries and who offends his ears daily during the rest of his wretched

---

[43]ibid, I, p149

life by her grammatical blunders. Obviously he has failed to find happiness.[44]

Two discrepancies are immediately evident here. Shenstone did not 'toy' with landscape gardening, he was one of its leading exponents and this portrayal of his 'housekeeper' bears no relation to the Mary Cutler described in Chapter 4 and to whom Dodsley sent a copy of his play *Cleone*.

As we know how highly Graves esteemed Shenstone, it is hard to know what he thought he was doing in even hinting at a parallel between his gifted and cultured friend and the coarse buffoon we meet with in the pages of what is not a 'novel'.

Mrs Betty, the housekeeper, is incapable of a single sentence without some malapropism: 'I am sure they were people of *extinction* by their *motions*.' And when the two friends eventually arrive at their destination (after 40 pages of picaresque *digression)* and meet up with Columella, no one would ever guess that this was meant to be William Shenstone:

> ... on opening the garden gate, they discovered their philosophical friend running across the lawn, with a faggot-stick is one hand, and a book in the other, his hair about his ears, and one stocking about his heels, in a most violent paroxysm of rage. 'D..mn 'em,' says Columella (the torrent of his passion getting the better of his politeness, and even his surprise at the sight of his old friends). 'D..mn 'em,' says he, 'these pigs have routed up all my primroses and periwinkles.'[45]

A touch of didacticism, a moral element, is not unexpected in any eighteenth-century work, but in *Columella* with its give-away sub-title or *The Distressed Anchoret* we get no further

[44]Tracey, p140
[45]*Columella*, I, p45-46

than page 3 before we are being preached at. We may as well be sitting in a pew as reading a book:

> But when a young person, after having been prepared by a liberal education, and a long and regular course of studies for some learned or ingenious profession, and qualified to be useful to the world in some eminent station; when such a one retires, in the vigour of life, through mere indolence or love of ease, and spends his days in solitude and inactivity ... such a one, I say, not only robs the community of a useful member ... but probably lays the foundation of his own infelicity; for he will not only find himself unqualified to that retirement of which he had formed such romantic ideas; but the consciousness of having deserted his proper station in society.[46]

Graves might well have saved himself and his readers a good deal of trouble if he had stopped there, but no, the same sermon is preached with the minimum of change in digression after digression. When one of the visitors offers to entertain the others with a story, it is a very long story with an obvious ending and the same obvious moral: industry is more godly than idleness. In Volume Two, when we are nearing the end, it is still the same: 'I am now persuaded that a life of mere indolence and inactivity, must in the end prove irksome and disgusting.'[47] It is simply the familiar Protestant work ethic, a retelling of the parable of Matthew 5:15, the hiding of a light under a bushel.

It would be possible to endorse the view that Shenstone did indeed dwindle into a *distressed anchoret* by citing 'Elegy XI' which bewails 'how soon the pleasing novelty of life is over', or 'Elegy XXIV' which recounts the 'imperfect pleasures of a solitary

---

[46]ibid, I, p46
[47]ibid, II, p171

life' but the *ubi sunt* element of the first and the stylised melancholy of the other should warn us against reading them as overtly personal statements.

Trundling through potted sermon after potted sermon in *Columella* and thinking back to the confident claims of those who favoured the equation $C = S$, one wonders how, if they ever reached the end, they could have come to such a conclusion. Sadly for their theory, but happily for Shenstone, he did not die of misery. But this negative conclusion still does not bring us any nearer to a positive statement as to who or what he was. Certainly there is no other figure in the whole of eighteenth-century literature to compare with him: he covers so many different genres and in each he is totally himself.

One thing worth noting is that no one ever speaks ill of him, save for the spiteful and elitist duo Gray and Walpole, whose opinions on this score can be safely ignored. What is certain is that on his death, many warm and moving tributes were paid to him, the most typical being that of Joseph Heely in his *Letters on the Beauties of ... The Leasowes* who celebrates:

> ... the hospitable, the generous and the immortal Shenstone! whose private character did so much honour to humanity; whose public one, in the literary world, as a poet, and a man of consummate knowledge, ranks so estimable; and to whose exquisite taste is wholly owing the inimitable beauties that rise in The Leasowes[48].

But the final word should be left to Thomas Whately, who described The Leasowes as being 'a perfect picture of his mind, simple, elegant and amiable'.[49]

---

[48]Heely, p.95
[49]Whately, p137

# BIBLIOGRAPHY

Auden, W.H. and Kronenberger, Louis, *The Faber Book of Aphorisms* (London, 1964)

Alpers, Paul, *What is Pastoral?* (University of Chicago Press, 1996)

Brooks, Cleanth, ed. *The Percy Letters* (Yale, 1977)

Brown, Jane, *My Darling Heriott* (London, 2006)

Curry, Neil, *Six Eighteenth-Century Poets* (London, 2011)

*William Cowper: A Revaluation (London, 2015)*

Duggan, Audrey, *The World of William Shenstone* (Studley, 2004)

*The Chequered Changes: A Portrait of Lady Luxborough,* (Studley, 2008)

Ellis, Havelock, ed, *Men and Manners* (New York 1927)

Friedman, Albert B, *The Ballad Revival* (Chicago, 1964)

Garfield, Simon, *To the Letter* (London, 2013)

Geary, James, *The World in a Phrase: A Brief History of the Aphorism* (London, 2001)

Gilfillan, Rev George, *The Poetical Works of William Shenstone* (Edinburgh, 1854)

Gifford, Terry, *Pastoral* (London, 1999)

Goldsmith, Oliver, *The History of a Poet's Garden,* Westminster Magazine, 1777.

Graves, Richard, *Recollection of Some Particulars in the Life of William Shenstone, Esq* (London, 1788)

*Columella,* (London, 1799)

Gray, Thomas, *The Letters, ed.* Duncan C. Tovey (London, 1909)

Heely, Joseph, Letters *on the Beauties of Hagley, Envill and The Leasowes* (London, 1777)

Hey, Colin, *The Warwickshire Coterie,* (1991)

Hull, Thomas, ed. *Select Letters Between the late Duchess of Somerset ... William Shenstone & Ohers.* (London, 1778)

Humphreys, A.R., *William Shenstone: An Eighteenth-Century Portrait* (Cambridge, 1937)

Hunt, John Dixon & Willis, Peter, eds. *The Genius of the Place* (London, 1988)

Hutton, William Holden, *The Burford Papers* (London 1905)

Johnson, Samuel, *Lives of the English Poets,* ed. G Birkbeck Hill (London, 1905)

Jung, Sandro, *Poetic Meaning in the Eighteenth-Century: Poems of Mark Akenside and William Shenstone* (Lampeter,2002)

Knox, Vicesimus, *Essays: Moral and Literary* (London, 1782)

Matthews, Stephen, *Josiah Relph of Sebergham: England's First Dialect Poet* (Carlisle, 2015)

Nokes, David, *Samuel Johnson: A Life* (London, 2010)

Purkis, E. Monro, *William Shenstone: Poet and Landscape Gardener* (*Wolverhampton, 1931*)

Redford, Bruce, *The Converse of the Pen* (Chicago, 1986)

Rymer, Thomas, *An Essay of Dramatic Poetry* (London, 1693)

Solomon, Harry S., *The Rise of Robert Dodsley* (Illinois, 1996)

Tierney, James E., (ed) *The Correspondence of Robert Dodsley* (Cambridge, 1988)

Tracy, Clarence, *A Portrait of Richard Graves* (Toronto, 1987)

Whately, Thomas, (ed Michael Symes) *Observations on Modern Gardening* (London, 2016)

Walpole, Horace, *Selected Letters* (New Haven, 1973)

 *On Modern Gardening* (London 1770)

Williams, Marjorie, *William Shenstone: A Chapter in Eighteenth Century Taste* (New York, 1935)

Williams, Marjorie, ed., *The Letters of William Shenstone* (Oxford, 1939)

# INDEX

Adams, John 143
Addison, Joseph 15, 24, 83, 90, 99, 100, 136-7
Alcock, Edward 80, 87, 157
Arne, Thomas 94
Arnold, Mary 82-85, 120
Attwood, Matthew 155
Auden, W.H. 46, 78-9

Baskerville, John 98, 110, 161
Bentley, Richard 105
Blake, William 80
Boswell, James 89 162
Boyle, Richard 136
Bridgeman, Charles 135
Brooks, Clarence 105
Burns, Robert 64

Chatterton, Thomas 103,107
Clare, John 99
Cole, William 169
Coleridge, Samuel 21, 108
Collins, William 72, 106
   Ode to Evening 92
Congreve, William 90
Cowley, Abraham 99

Cowper, William 16, 72, 112, 121
Cutler, Mary 82-85, 151, 173

Dalton, John 29
Darwin, Charles 74
Davie, Donald 50, 74
Defoe, Daniel 172
Dodsley, Robert 16, 20-22, 41, 50, 54, 59, 67, 75, 76, 83, 89-143, 161, 166, 168
Dodsley, James 113
Dolman, Maria 140, 151
Duck, Stephen 90
Dudley, Council 155
Duggan, Audrey 170
Dyer, John
   *The Fleece* 91
   *Grongar Hill* 92

Fielding, Henry 15, 112
Friedman, Albert B. 105

Garrick, David 95-6
Gay, John 97
Geary, James 77-8

Gifford, Terry 71

Gilfillan, George 75, 114, 168, 170

Goldsmith, Oliver 56, 58, 154,

Grainger, James 104

Gray, Thomas 50, 57, 91-93, 105,112, 113, 122, 129, 163, 168, 175

Graves, Richard 18, 19, 21, 27, 30, 36-42, 54, 59, 61, 68, 84, 94, 96, 110, 139, 140-1, 148, 158, 160-2

  *Recollections of Some Particulars in the Life of William Shenstone* 19, 40, 148, 158

  *The Spiritual Quixote* 39-40, 149,158

  *Columella* 40, 84, 170-175

Halesowen, 17, 39, 123, 144, 151, 155, 160, 166

Halliday, Francis 154

Hardy, Thomas 94

Hammond, James

  *Love's Elegies* 66

Hazlitt, William 50

Heeley, Joseph 148, 151, 175

Henry VIII 111

Hertford, Francis 29

Horne, Edward 154

Hull, Thomas 123, 165

Hylton, John Scott 146

Jago, Richard 17, 19, 21, 23, 27, 31-36, 41, 49, 80, 91, 92, 94, 110, 118, 158, 161

Jefferson, Thomas 143

Johnson, Samuel 11, 17, 20, 21, 23, 24, 25, 32, 40, 44, 46, 47, 50, 53. 60, 62, 63, 65, 66, 78, 82, 83, 89, 91, 100, 106, 108 114, 142, 143, 161, 163, 168, 170, 171

Jago, Richard 17, 19, 20-26, 32, 40, 44, 46, 47, 49, 51, 53, 54, 72, 80, 91, 92, 94, 109, 110, 115, 118, 119, 120, 127, 140, 158, 159, 161, 165-167

Jonson, Ben 12

Keats, John 49

Kent, William 136-137

Knox, Vicesimus 107

Knight, Robert 29, 31

The Leasowes, 17, 18, 21, 27, 31, 37, 58, 61, 63, 80, 81, 97, 98, 118, 119, 127, 130,139-155, 160-170, 175

Levens Hall, 133, 136

Lloyd, Sarah 17, 53, 54, 57, 58

Louis XIV 135

Luxborough, Lady Henrietta 20, 26, 27-31, 41, 63, 85, 94, 110, 116-122, 124-131, 142 146, 148, 150, 153, 161, 170

Lyttleton, Sir George 91, 142, 145, 154

Macpherson, James
  *Ossian* 103

Matthews, Stephen 106

Marvell, Andrew 12

Milton, John *Lycidas* 66

Montaigne, Michael 156

Montagu, Lady Mary 110, 112

Moore, Edward 97

Mowl, Timothy 154

Miller, Sanderson 145

Nash, Treadway Russell
  *Collections for the History of
  Worcestershire* 36

Nietzsche, Frederick 78

Pepys, Samuel 104

Percy, Thomas 21, 98-110, 161

Pembroke College, 17, 32, 37,
  41, 159

Pomfret, John
  *The Choice* 11-14

Pope, Alexander 14-16, 21, 24,
  27, 28, 34, 52, 53, 59, 60, 66,
  73, 74, 78, 86, 87, 88, 90-92,
  99, 104 110, 112, 122, 136,
  161

Relph, Josiah 106

Richardson, Samuel 97, 112, 172

Rochefoucauld 106

Rochester, John Wilmot 28

Ross, Thomas 157

Rowe, Elizabeth 29

Ruskin, John 70-71, 147

Schlegal, Frederick 78

Shenstone, William
  Brief biography 17-22
  Letters 113-128
  *Colemira,* 47-348, 50
  *Elegies* 64-74, 95, 174
  *Eclogues* 47, 151-2,
  *The Judgement of Hercules* 20,
  50, 58, 91
  *Men and Manners,* 75-88
  *Pastoral Ballad* 20, 61-64
  *Poems on Several Occasions* 18,
  50
  *The School-Mistress* 17, 20, 50-
  58, 91-92, 97, 116, 169
  Songs 59
  *To a Friend,* 48-50
  *Unconnected Thoughts on
  Gardening* 144-146, 152
  *Written at an Inn* 44-47

Sidney, Sir Philip 67

Smart, Christopher 14, 72, 97

Somervile, William 21, 23-27,
  31, 35, 41, 94, 116, 128, 148

Steele, Richard 90

Spenser, Edmund 51

Steele, Richard 90

Sterne, Laurence 171

Stukely, William 105

Swift, Jonathan 110, 172

Symes, Michael 153

Temple, William135

Turnbull, Alexander 110

Theobald, Lewis 104

Thomas, R.S. 48

Thomson, James 15, 16, 21, 24,
    29, 34, 57, 74, 92, 122, 152,
    142 163

Thrale, Henrietta 143

Tracey, Clemence 172


Villa d'Este 134

Vindolanda 111


Walpole, Horace 29, 50, 59,
    107, 110, 112, 118, 134-137,
    169, 170, 175

Wharton, Thomas 104, 106, 110

Whistler, Anthony 21, 27, 41-44,
    46, 82, 94, 110, 114, 160

Wittgenstein, Ludwig 78

Woodhouse, James 81, 153, 162,
    163

Wordsworth, William 21, 58, 64,
    70, 71, 108